Praise for *Heal the Witch W*

T0023385

"Celeste Larsen has written a powerful book addr
that so many seekers of magic have to deal with throughout their
journey. In *Heal the Witch Wound*, we are reminded of the persecutions
and harassment that those who practiced magic were forced to endure,
with the addition of modern perspectives that will resonate with a new
generation of witches. Most of all, in uncovering and articulating these
wounds, Larsen illuminates a path to deep healing. This one should be
on any magic lover's shelf!"

—Briana Saussy, author of *Making Magic*

"Even now, the witch wound still bleeds, and many of those who choose
to claim the name *witch* are accepting an invitation to heal this soul-
injury. Healing the witch wound can only happen when the history
is examined; in the absence of such accounting, the healing becomes
a fruitless pursuit. With the understanding of how the witch wound
is inextricably linked to the horrors of capitalism and colonization,
healing this centuries-old wound becomes the most potent shadow
work a witch can do. Celeste Larsen's *Heal the Witch Wound* is a rare
achievement that discusses the witch wound with historical depth and
also offers practical invitations to heal the wound on a personal and
collective level. It is an essential addition to any witch's library."

—Danielle Dulsky, author of *The Holy Wild*

"In *Heal the Witch Wound*, Celeste Larsen addresses a topic that every
witch needs to examine at some point: reconciling the word and concept
of *witch* with its deeply complicated history. Celeste explores how to
process the tension of self-identifying as 'other' in a society that depends
on labels and imposed boundaries. And she provides rituals, exercises,
journal prompts, and meditations to uncover and work through
feelings of reticence, uncertainty, and fear to help you affirm your own
authenticity and expression as a witch."

—Arin Murphy-Hiscock, author of *The Green Witch*

"*Heal the Witch Wound* offers an insightful perspective on the historical causes of the trauma that many self-identified witches experience to this day. But more than that, it is a call to action!—not only to heal ourselves of past intergenerational trauma but also to lovingly and openly accept ourselves as witches. With a better understanding of our shared witch wound, we can work toward healing it, collectively."

—@witchofcolorado

"Do you ever find yourself hiding your tarot practice from family members, downplaying your love of astrology, or feeling like a freak for being a witch? In *Heal the Witch Wound*, Celeste Larsen normalizes such feelings. Larsen starts with a history of the witch hunts and ends by offering accessible but effective rituals to help work through the ancestral trauma they have caused and step into your magick."

—Sophie Saint Thomas, author of *The Glamour Witch*

"Celeste Larsen provides an informative overview of the history and struggles of past witches, while also offering guidance and inspiration for those seeking to embark on a magical journey of healing and self-discovery. By deepening our connection to the natural world and reconnecting with the self, readers can gain a deeper understanding of their own personal power and discover a nourishing spiritual path."

—Leah Middleton, creator of *The Redheaded Witch*

HEAL THE

WITCH WOUND

Reclaim Your Magic and Step Into Your Power

CELESTE LARSEN

WEISER BOOKS

This edition first published in 2023 by Weiser Books, an imprint of
Red Wheel/Weiser, LLC

With offices at:
65 Parker Street, Suite 7
Newburyport, MA 01950
www.redwheelweiser.com

ISBN 978-1-57863-798-0

Library of Congress Cataloging-in-Publication Data

Names: Larsen, Celeste, author.
Title: Heal the witch wound : reclaim your magic and step into your power /
    Celeste Larsen.
Description: Newburyport, MA : Weiser Books, 2023. | Includes bibliographical
    references. | Summary: "The 'witch wound' is a collective, intergenerational, psychic
    wound that has scarred people, mostly women, for centuries. The roots of this
    wound run deep, going back to the historical witch hunts, the 'Burning Times,' when
    tens of thousands of innocent individuals were accused of practicing malicious magic
    and executed in the most inhumane ways. In this book, the author guides modern
    witches (as well as pagans, energy workers, occultists, and other spiritual individuals)
    on the path to healing the witch wound by demystifying this dark era in history,
    exploring the most common signs and symptoms of the witch wound, and using
    step-by-step rituals, exercises, journal prompts, affirmations, visualizations, and
    other tools to heal the wound"—Provided by publisher.
Identifiers: LCCN 2022050504 | ISBN 9781578637980 (paperback) |
    ISBN 9781633412958 (kindle edition)
Subjects: LCSH: Witchcraft. | Occultism. | Magic.
Classification: LCC BF1571 .L37 2023 | DDC 133.4/3—dc23/eng/20221223 LC
    record available at *https://lccn.loc.gov/2022050504*

Cover design by Sky Peck Design
Interior by Debby Dutton
Typeset in Adobe Jenson and Frutiger LT

Printed in the United States of America
IBI
10 9 8 7 6 5 4 3 2 1

To Saturn,
for reminding me who I was born to be.

To my family,
for always believing in my magic.

And to those who lost their lives in the witch hunts;
you are not forgotten.

CONTENTS

Introduction   ix

Part One: The Burning Times   1

   1. Before the Burning Times   3
   2. The Peak of the Witch Trials   11
   3. The Role of Gender in the Witch Trials 19
   4. The Legacy of the Witch Craze   25

Part Two: Symptoms of the Witch Wound   33

   5. Hiding in the Spiritual Broom Closet   35
   6. Muting Your Self-Expression   45
   7. Feeling Lost, Stuck, or Blocked   55
   8. Ancestral Wounding and Past-Life Memories 67
   9. The Wounded Feminine   77

Part Three: Healing the Witch Wound   87

   10. Clearing Energetic Space   89
   11. Conjuring Self-Empowerment   103
   12. Ancestral Healing   117
   13. Healing the Divine Feminine   127
   14. Somatic Healing   141
   15. Earth Healing   151
   16. Moving into Your Magic and Power   165

The Spiral Path of the Witch   179

Notes   181

Bibliography   187

INTRODUCTION

You were born to live a magical life. Deep within your soul, you *know* this; it is why you picked up this book. But there is another reason why you now hold this book in your hands: because some part of you feels it is unsafe to fully embrace the magic that exists within and around you. This part of you carries an age-old wound—one that keeps you from claiming your magic, owning your power, and shining fearlessly in your truth.

The *witch wound* is a collective, intergenerational, psychic wound that is rooted in the Burning Times—an era of widespread persecution and violence against suspected witches. You may already be familiar with some of the most famous witch hunts, such as the Pendle or Salem witch trials. During this period, tens of thousands of innocent people were accused of practicing malicious magic and massacred in some of the most inhumane ways imaginable. But there is more to this dark era than meets the eye. Though most of its stories remain untold, the deep-seated effects on society remain.

The impact of the witch hunts has reverberated through time and space, altering our collective unconscious—the shared beliefs and ideas that connect us all—and affecting the lives of spiritual individuals in modern times. If you are among the many who carry the witch wound, you may find yourself hiding your spiritual beliefs and magical practices out of fear of being judged, shamed, mocked, vilified, or rejected. You may feel it is unsafe to speak your mind and be seen for who you really are, or you might struggle to fit in while being true to yourself. You may have strong feelings of doubt, guilt, and shame about your intuitive abilities. You may dream of sharing your unique gifts and creative expressions with the world, but dimming your own light feels safer than letting it shine. You may even have past-life or ancestral memories of being persecuted for witchcraft during the Burning Times.

The witch wound runs much deeper than simple fear or insecurity; it operates on a subconscious level within the nervous system itself, passed down to us through generations. It is also embedded in our culture and reinforced daily through the systems of patriarchy, capitalism, imperialism, colonialism, and religious intolerance. Magic and nature-based spirituality cannot be easily controlled by those who built these oppressive systems, so instead, they are devalued and villainized.

Have you ever noticed how certain spiritual concepts are socially acceptable, while others are not? Nobody bats an eye when somebody prays to God, but if you tell the average person that you cast spells, there is a strong chance they will respond with judgment or contempt. This is the witch wound at work on a societal level. Individually, this can show up as feeling like you are "crazy" or "weird" for believing in energies, spirits, and magic. You aren't. We have all just become so disconnected from our innate spirituality that we have forgotten that *everyone* can tap into magical perspectives and abilities.

Healing the witch wound is not about going back in time or dwelling on the atrocities of the past—quite the opposite. This work is about taking steps now to reclaim your power, live a more magical life, and embody your most authentic self. For many, healing the witch wound is a lifelong journey complete with new beginnings, obstacles, missteps, self-discovery and ultimately deep fulfillment and validation. As you progress along this journey, you will learn practices to work through your limiting beliefs, find empowerment within, and break the cycle of fear, shame, and guilt in your lineage—and in doing so benefit society as a whole.

When you rise to meet this challenge, the impact of your actions stretches far beyond your own life. The witch wound causes us to shrink ourselves, hide our magic, and deprive the world of our gifts—the very gifts that someone, somewhere, is praying and waiting for in this moment. By tending to your spiritual wounds and working through personal blockages, you create expansion and widen your opportunities to heal others with your unique expression of magic, creativity, and wisdom. This is the path of the wounded healer—one who gives to others what they themselves most needed when they were lost and hurting. It's a path I myself walk.

I was inspired to write this book after awakening to the reality of my own witch wound and learning to tend to it through my own emotional alchemy. As the legendary philosopher's stone is said to transmute common metals into gold, the healing tools I acquired along this journey of magic and empowerment alchemized the feelings and beliefs that were holding me back into new emotions that instead propelled me forward: Anxiety became curiosity. Grief morphed into empathy. Loneliness grew to connection, and rage transformed into passion. Now, I seek to share these healing tools, practices, and rituals with you.

We'll explore the wisdom of this book through the framework of that most magical of numbers—three. Part one journeys back in history to the dark era of the Burning Times. This is a painful time to revisit, yet its memory holds important context and clues about how and why the witch wound continues to manifest today. Part two is firmly rooted in the present moment and explores the most common signs and symptoms of the witch wound. Part three branches into the bright and brilliant future, offering rituals, exercises, and other tools for self-healing. Over the course of this book, we will weave these three threads of past, present, and future into a holistic understanding of the witch wound.

What Is a Witch?

I am a witch, and if you've felt called to pick up this book, there is a good chance that you are too. Perhaps *witch* is a term you have been using to refer to your spiritual and magical practices for years, or maybe this is the first time you have ever been asked to think about yourself in this way. If you fall into the latter category, you are certainly not alone. After all, the word witch is more commonly used as an insult than a compliment in our culture, even among many spiritual folks.

Centuries' worth of fairy tales, movies, TV shows, novels, and history itself have taught us to fear the witch—to see her (because according to the trope, it's always a "her") as a villain, a monster, something to defend against and defeat. Even in media that portray witches in a positive light, they are still presented as outcasts who are forced to hide their gifts or struggle to coexist with nonmagical folks. The witch is the ultimate Other. This was the mindset that fanned the flames of the Burning Times, when tens of thousands of individuals were violently persecuted based on the belief that they were practicing witchcraft. While most of these individuals were, in fact, *not* witches—as we will explore later—many of them did fall under the category of "other." The victims of the Burning Times were women, elderly widows, the poor, the unhoused, non-Christians, and people with disabilities. And certainly, some of them were keepers of the old ways—healers, midwives, diviners, seers, cunning folk. In all cases, their persecutors were fearful, hateful, and power-hungry. It is a tale as old as time.

Yet isn't it strange how we were all taught to fear these supposed witches who were burned alive rather than the men who started the fires? This, of course, is because history is written by the victors. This truth is readily apparent in the way we are taught about the witch trials. Even in modern lessons, there is an air of horror and mystery. *Were they really witches? Did they deserve their fates? Who knows . . .?*

Today we are plagued by numerous stereotypes and misconceptions about witches. These falsities harm the millions who are actually interested in using witchcraft as a tool to enchant and empower their lives. And ultimately, that is the core of what it means to be a witch. While many definitions of witch have been proposed, this is mine: a witch is someone who claims magic as their birthright and uses it to create change in their inner and outer worlds.

Yes, magic is your birthright. It is untrue that some people are born as witches and others are not. Unlike in the many fictional worlds where witches reside, in our world we are all born with the ability to tap into our innate spirituality and magic. This is our Earth-given right as humans. Cultural conditioning can cause us to lose touch with this birthright, but we are all capable of reclaiming it and owning our spiritual, magical side. This is what it means to be a witch and why this path is open to anyone and everyone. As long as you identify with and claim the title, then *you are a witch*.

And if you don't claim that title? That is perfectly fine too. Perhaps you identify with the archetype of the witch, but don't quite feel comfortable applying that label to your spiritual practice. Whether you self-identify as a witch or not, trust that you have picked up this book for a reason and this is the next step in your spiritual journey.

As you walk the path of healing the witch wound, you may find yourself feeling more open to the world of witches, witchcraft, and magic—after all, such hesitations are one of the key symptoms of the witch wound. You may also discover that there is another term that feels right in your own body, such as healer, energy worker, pagan, mage, empath, intuitive, or spiritual seeker. My goal is not to steer you toward any one path, but rather to guide you as you explore your own relationship with your inner witch.

How to Use This Book

First, a brief note about what this book is *not:* this book is not a substitute for professional therapy, counseling, or trauma healing. Many of the symptoms of the witch wound can be similar to those of other unhealed traumas and mental illnesses, which should be managed under the supervision of a qualified expert. The work outlined in this book cannot take the place of treatments such as therapy and prescribed medications.

What this book *is*: this book is an initiation into the work of healing the witch wound. It is an ally for your journey inward, guiding and encouraging you as you navigate the shadowy depths of this psychic trauma. These words provide the framework for alchemizing your witch wound into your power, but you are the alchemist. Without your magic and intention, the healing cannot happen.

As you read, allow yourself the space and time to process your emotions as they arise. When you come across a statement or story that awakens something within you, pause. Sit with that feeling, breathe into it, expand it, study it. What emotions, thoughts, memories, and body sensations occur? For many, this can be the most challenging part of the work. We have been taught to distrust our bodies, our emotions, and our intuition—to mute those internal alarm bells that are meant to keep us safe in favor of more "rational" social constructs.

But this inner wisdom is the true medicine, so please, don't rush this part of the process. When you read a sentence that touches your spirit or sends chills across your body, stop and listen. When you encounter a historical fact that causes your stomach to churn or your throat to tighten, stop and listen. When your body begs you to cry, to laugh, to dance, to scream, to be gentle with yourself—trust that this wisdom is coming from a deeply connected place.

And when you begin integrating these insights in your day-to-day life, that is when the healing happens. Each time you notice one of your triggers and take a different action than you normally would—such as speaking up when you would typically stay silent, even when you feel afraid—your brain creates new neural pathways based on this behavior. Over time, as you repeat these new behaviors and these pathways become stronger, you can successfully rewire your brain with thoughts and beliefs that support you in your journey toward personal empowerment. This is known as neuroplasticity, and we'll be exploring it through the lens of magic and spirituality.

These pages will lead you through a diverse range of practices, from spells and rituals to more mundane exercises. That is because this book was written for everyone who feels called to this work, regardless of experience level. There are no prerequisites such as belonging to a certain witchcraft tradition or spiritual belief system. Some practices may not resonate for you, but might be deeply impactful for someone else. Take what works, adapt and customize where you can, and leave the rest. This is your journey.

Grant yourself the space to get curious and follow the threads of your emotions and your imagination as you read, weaving together your own theories and self-healing processes. This book is a lifeline, not a tether. It will always be here to ground and center you should you get lost along the way, but it should never hold you back.

Trust that you are ready for this work, that you are divinely guided and protected, and that you are not alone. You are part of a circle of well and wise witches that stretches around the globe—witches of all ages, nationalities, races, genders, religious backgrounds, and spiritual paths embarking on this journey alongside you.

It is time for your inner exploration to commence. It is time to heal your witch wound, reclaim your magic, and step into your power.

Part One

THE BURNING TIMES

Between the fifteenth and eighteenth centuries, tens of thousands of individuals throughout Europe were executed for the crime of witch-craft. Most modern scholars place the approximate number of persons executed around 50,000, though estimates of over 100,000 deaths have been proposed. Countless more—perhaps twice the number of those executed—were accused, tortured, and exiled by their communities. Of those prosecuted for witchcraft during these so-called Burning Times, roughly 80 percent were women, many over the age of forty. Burning at the stake was indeed the most common method of execution in the regions where the most tyrannical witch hunts took place, but behead-ing, hanging, and drowning were also widely used by witch-hunters and executioners.

These words are difficult to read, and I must warn you that the sto-ries and facts contained within the following pages will only become more harrowing. Nevertheless, for many modern witches, facing and holding space for the horrors of the past can be a deeply cathartic process that sheds light on how and why the witch wound is showing up in their own bodies. This has certainly been true in my experience; by coming to terms with the atrocities inflicted upon accused witches in early modern

Europe—in the lands where my not-so-distant ancestors lived—I have gained a deeper understanding and validation of the intergenerational trauma within my own body and psyche. This is the medicine I hope to offer you in the process of healing your own witch wound.

Yet you know your heart, mind, and body far better than I do. Before you continue onward through part one, I lovingly urge you to become the master of your healing journey. These words are your guide, but only along the paths you *choose to follow*. If something within you is telling you the time is not right to dive into these depths—that learning about the barbarities of the Burning Times would retraumatize you and shut down your capacity to heal rather than expanding it—then trust that instinct. There is much to be gained from each of the three sections of this book, and should you choose to bypass this one, these pages can still prepare you to rise into the powerful magic your soul is calling you to.

Should you choose to venture into the dark history of the Burning Times, I ask you likewise to become the master of your own journey. If certain facts or stories feel particularly painful or triggering, grant yourself the time and space to sit with those feelings. Take your time noticing whatever arises within you—grief, sorrow, fear, disgust, anger, rage. These emotions are your highest self's way of pointing you toward the aspects of the witch wound that need healing. Embark upon this journey with an open mind and without self-judgment. Be gentle with yourself and take breaks from reading as needed.

Inhale deeply—pause, for there is magic in this space between—and exhale fully.

Let's begin.

1

Before the Burning Times

What spurred the dramatic rise in witchcraft accusations in Europe of the fifteenth, sixteenth, and seventeenth centuries? To understand this, we must first journey back further in time to the Middle Ages. According to the canon law of the Catholic Church during the Middle Ages—specifically, to a body of text known as *Canon Episcopi*—witches and magic did not exist.

The Church's official viewpoint was that while the Devil was real and had the ability to possess the minds of women—who were considered to be more susceptible to the influences of evil—any woman who actually believed herself to be a witch was simply dreaming or suffering from delusions. Similarly, anyone who claimed that witches existed and wielded real power was deemed guilty of heresy and succumbing to pagan superstitions. And this position is reflected in the actions of religious and political leaders of the time, such as when Pope Gregory VII wrote to King Harald III of Denmark in 1080 *forbidding* the execution of suspected witches.

Views on magic and witchcraft began to shift during the Late Middle Ages, in the period between 1250 and 1500. Europe faced multiple crises during the fourteenth and fifteenth centuries that rocked the foundations of society and led to major upheavals in politics, religion, and culture. A period of regional cooling known as the Little Ice Age occurred between 1300 and 1850, resulting in longer, colder, harsher winters and poorer harvests. Excessive rain and snow at the time led to widespread crop failures, malnutrition, and economic downturn. Between 1315 and 1317, the Great Famine reduced Europe's population by an estimated 10 percent. One major disaster followed another: as the bubonic plague pandemic swept across Europe beginning in 1347, the Black Death claimed the lives of one-third of all Europeans.

As the various crises of the Late Middle Ages ravaged the European continent, the wage gap between the wealthy and the poor widened. Following the Great Famine and the Black Death, the surviving landowners and wealthy farmers began acquiring more land and removing it from communal use by constructing fences in a process known as enclosure. While this increased the value of the land for those who owned it, their tenants were forced off the once-common areas their families had cultivated and depended upon for generations.

In a tale as old as time, the rich became richer and the poor became poorer. As enclosure systems, taxation, inflation, and food scarcity increased, so did working-class rebellions against the nobility. Older women and widows were disproportionately harmed by the privatization of land and were among the most vocal dissenters. Many of them turned to begging, which came to be seen as a nuisance and sparked fear of retaliation among those neighbors who refused to help. Others took a bolder approach by participating in enclosure riots, speaking out against those in power, and publicly cursing those who denied them aid.[1]

Meanwhile, certain religious philosophers and leaders were working to reshape the Catholic Church's views on witches and magic. During the thirteenth century, the Dominican friar Thomas Aquinas published works disputing the commonly held belief that witchcraft was not real, as the *Canon Episcopi* had maintained. Aquinas argued that it was possible for individuals to collaborate with the Devil and to obtain certain magical abilities, which could be used for evil purposes. His works were cited more than one hundred times in a now-infamous book published by the German inquisitor Heinrich Kramer in 1486—the most widely distributed witch-hunting handbook in history.

The Hammer of the Witches

In 1485, an Austrian woman named Helena Scheuberin stood trial in Innsbruck for the offense of using baneful magic to murder a knight. Her trial was overseen by the inquisitor Heinrich Kramer. During the trial, Kramer emphasized Scheuberin's sexual history and promiscuity rather than her magical abilities—an argument the court did not find compelling.

Much to Kramer's dismay, Scheuberin was acquitted of the charges and released. Angry and humiliated by his defeat, he began writing a treatise on witchcraft defending his methods of identifying witches—a work that would later become the *Malleus Maleficarum*, translated as Hammer of the Witches. This book consists of three sections: The first argues that witchcraft is indeed real, that those who deny its reality are guilty of heresy, that witches are inherently linked with the Devil, and that women are more inclined toward witchcraft than men. The second part describes the "evils of witchcraft" in ghastly detail, outlining the specific ways witches may harm those around them—destroying crops, conjuring storms, transforming men into beasts, devouring children—and offering remedies for those affected by witchcraft. The third and final section of the Malleus Maleficarum describes the recommended method of prosecuting witches, including how to identify, interrogate, and execute them. Kramer's justification for the cruel and gruesome methods of witch-hunting outlined in the book can be found in the short yet impactful Bible verse Exodus 22:18: "Thou shalt not suffer a witch to live."

From beginning to conclusion, this work preys on the fears of both commoners and nobles by providing "evidence" of the deeply disturbing, grotesque, and terrifying activities of Devil-worshipping witches. In one chapter, an imprisoned woman describes the manner in which she and her coven would murder unbaptized children: "With our spells we kill them in their cradles or even when they are sleeping by their parents' side, in such a way that they afterwards are thought to have been overlain or to have died some other natural death."[2] The witch then recounts in gruesome detail how the children would be secretly retrieved from their graves, cooked in cauldrons, and eaten.

Confessions like this one served two purposes: to ignite the imagination of a God-fearing society with a collective memory of famines, plagues, poverty, and death and to make it impossible for those accused to defend themselves. What possible explanation could a woman give against the charge of using evil magic to murder a child, when the only evidence against her would be that a child should die of seemingly natural causes and vague claims of the accused having been jealous, bitter, or angry?

If there is any doubt that the *Malleus Maleficarum* was written to incite terror and to strengthen the influence of patriarchy and oppressive religion, we need only to look to chapter 7 of part II, question I, in which the entirety of the text is devoted to describing how a witch can use spells to make a man's sexual organs disappear. "For a certain man tells that, when he had lost his member, he approached a known witch to ask her to restore it to him. She told the afflicted man to climb a certain tree, and that he might take which he liked out of a nest in which there were several members. And when he tried to take a big one, the witch said: You must not take that one; adding, because it belonged to a parish priest."[3]

For a period of two centuries, the *Malleus Maleficarum* sold more copies than any book in Europe other than the Bible. Its impact would echo through the ages, and its words would go on to influence witch-hunters on the European continent—and eventually across the Atlantic in the American colonies—for more than three hundred years. Importantly, the Malleus Maleficarum shaped the course of the European witch craze in three ways: by proselytizing the belief that witches were real, dangerous, and evil; by maintaining that God would not permit an innocent person to be convicted of witchcraft, and thus barbaric forms of torture and execution were appropriate; and by furthering the idea that women were more susceptible to the Devil's influence than men and that it was necessary to discriminate against them.

Women in the Middle Ages

Before we progress into the era of the witch craze, let us take a moment to understand the roles of women in the period leading up to these times. Throughout most of the thousand-year period known as the Middle Ages, women enjoyed a surprising amount of independence. There was less division of labor than might be expected, especially within the working class.

In addition to their roles as wives, mothers, and homemakers, most medieval women earned their own income as spinners, seamstresses, brewers, midwives, healers, fortune-tellers, innkeepers, launderers, domestic servants, and wet nurses. Wealthy women had the opportunity to become educated and work as merchants, moneylenders, writers, and artisans and could participate in guilds. Unmarried women with few other resources could leverage their bodies to earn a living through sex work. Some of these women even came to own their own brothels.[4]

Perhaps the most significant socioeconomic contribution of women during the medieval era was with healing. Doctors were rare outside the largest cities, and in rural areas it was female healers who provided most of the medical care—much of which had origins in pagan folk magic. Herbal remedies were used to treat a diverse range of ailments, from infections and disease to impotence and difficult childbirth. As part of their healing rituals, wisewomen repeated charms and incantations, prepared amulets and potions containing powdered herbs and other ingredients, and performed divination. While some religious folks may have feared the power and wisdom these cunning women held, the majority of the common people depended heavily on them and respected them as members of the community.[5]

Importantly, the average medieval woman also lived much of her life in the company of other women, and it was women who formed her inner circle of day-to-day social interactions. Collectively, women raised babies and tended to various chores around the home. They also gathered socially during leisure time; the tavern was a popular place for working-class medieval women to talk, eat, drink wine, and dance—without the company of their husbands.[6] The strong bonds of friendship formed by medieval women—combined with their ability to earn income independently of their husbands—no doubt threatened the growing systems of capitalism and patriarchy in the Late Middle Ages.

After all, capitalism as a system relies on control and exploitation of the laborer and what they can produce, and women have an intrinsic power that naturally resists external control and exploitation: the life-creating capacities for pregnancy and childbirth. For thousands of years, women's bodies were celebrated and venerated as symbols of the divine generative force. Yet in a capitalist and patriarchal society, the sacred ability to create life puts a target on the back of every woman of childbearing age.[7]

A woman who chose to learn a trade and earn her own income—particularly a "feminine art" like divination or midwifery—rather than marrying and bearing children threatened patriarchal and capitalist structures in two ways: by refusing to use her sexuality as a tool for capitalism (i.e., procreating male offspring to populate the workforce) and by daring to be independent in a society that increasingly commanded her to be subservient to men.[8]

In 1547, a proclamation was issued in England forbidding women from enjoying their previous social freedoms and ordering men to keep their wives inside the home.[9] Similar decrees sprang up throughout Europe as mistrust and disdain for women—especially those who held power in their local communities or who spoke out against socioeconomic inequalities—spread across the continent. If the *Malleus Maleficarum* was the match that sparked the Burning Times, it was the gradual degradation of women and their place in society that served as the kindling.

The Witch Trials and Antisemitism

There is one last critical factor we must examine to understand why the witch craze burned across Europe with such ferocity, and that is the strong link between the persecution of suspected witches and the persecution of Jews. Indeed, many early modern stereotypes about how witches looked and behaved were rooted in a long history of antisemitism. Before the Church turned its attention to witches, heretics and Jews were its primary targets.

Throughout the Middle Ages, Jews were subjected to horrific forms of violence and discrimination. Like witches, they were blamed for many of the crises and misfortunes of the era; like women, they were increasingly barred from participating in guilds and other rights of citizenship. The Church believed Jews to have "putrid blood," which could only be cured by consuming the blood of a Christian.[10] Mass killings of Jews occurred throughout the period between 1000 and 1400, and were especially concentrated in German regions—a theme we will see reflected later during the witch trials.[11]

In 1215, the Fourth Lateran Council established a number of canons (i.e., rules and regulations), many of which centered around Judaism. Among these was a law stating that Jews must identify themselves by wearing special clothing, including a *Judenhut* or "Jewish hat." This pointed, cone-shaped hat with a circular brim was meant to make it easier for Christians to identify Jews—and thus opened opportunities to discriminate against them. In woodcut illustrations from this time, Jews were often depicted wearing the Judenhut and displaying monstrous features like horns and claws—symbolic of their supposed relationship with Satan.[12] Furthermore, because the Jewish Shabbat or Sabbath was a non-Christian ritualistic gathering, it was viewed as heretical, satanic, and depraved. Jews were accused of desecrating the host, sacrificing children, and fornicating with the Devil at these gatherings.

Pointed hats, unholy Sabbaths, cannibalism, ritual sacrifice, ties to Satan, sexual depravity—to anyone who has seen the stereotypical medieval image of a witch or has a basic understanding of the contents of the *Malleus Maleficarum*, these descriptors will no doubt sound familiar. This is no mere coincidence. In fact, Heinrich Kramer based the *Malleus Maleficarum* on an earlier work with a similar name: *Malleus Judeorum* (or Hammer of the Jews), published around 1420 by the inquisitor John of Frankfurt.[13] Additionally, a decade before publishing the *Malleus Maleficarum*, Kramer was directly involved in a trial of Jews in Turin—an experience that clearly influenced his point of view and messaging. In the *Malleus Maleficarum*, he writes that "the heresy of witches is the most heinous of the three degrees of infidelity," with that of Jews being second and of pagans being third.[14]

What shifted the Inquisition's focus from Jews and heretics to witches—and in particular, female witches? Many historians credit the printing press, which was invented a few decades before the *Malleus Maleficarum* was published. This enabled misogynistic witch-hunting propaganda to be shared farther and wider than it had ever been before, which incited mass witchcraft hysteria on the European continent.

Ultimately, the witch craze was not the result of just one single factor. Rather, it was a conglomeration of influences that worked together over the span of hundreds of years to shape early modern Europe into the ideal environment for a continent-wide witch hunt: misogyny, patriarchy, religious tyranny, scapegoating, land disputes, the rise of capitalism, shifting views about magic, political propaganda, and an established history of persecution and violence.

2

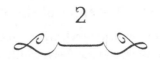

The Peak of the
Witch Trials

Following the publication of the *Malleus Maleficarum*, a wave of witch hunts swept across Europe. While it is impossible to pinpoint the true chronological start of the Burning Times, the first great witch trial in Germany—the Wiesensteig witch trial, which took place from 1562 to 1563—is commonly cited as the beginning of the early modern European witch craze.[1] (Note: For ease of understanding, this book generally refers to areas using modern-day national borders.)

Like much of the European continent, this small German town was ravaged by disease, famine, natural disasters, and political and religious turmoil during the early to mid-sixteenth century. After a particularly severe hailstorm in August of 1562 that ruined much of the year's wine crop, the town's overlord identified the apparent culprit of Wiesensteig's misfortune: witches. Within a matter of days, multiple townswomen were arrested, tortured, and executed for inflicting malicious magic upon Wiesensteig. By the end of that same year, an anonymous pamphlet titled *The True and Horrifying Deeds and Activities of Sixty-Three Witches, Who Have Been Executed By Fire in Wiesensteig* was printed and began circulating through Southern Germany.

Germany: The Epicenter of the Witch Craze

The atrocities of other German witch trials—including those in Trier, Fulda, Eichstätt, Würzburg, and Bamberg, which were among the largest in history—are no less nightmarish. In the lands of the archbishop of Trier, one thousand individuals from twenty-two villages were burned alive between 1587 and 1593, and two of the region's villages were left with just one female inhabitant each.[2] As in Wiesensteig, the Trier trials were preceded by a long succession of remarkably poor grain and wine harvests.

The trials of nearby Bamberg were unique in that many of the accused were public officials and members of the elite class, including the city's own mayor, Johannes Junius. After vehemently denying all charges of witchcraft for more than a week, during which time he was subjected to horrific forms of torture, Junius at last confessed on July 5, 1628, that he had renounced God for the Devil, attended the Witches' Sabbath, and buried a holy wafer of the Eucharist in an act of blasphemy. One month later, he was publicly burned alive. Yet the mayor's confession, vivid and detailed as it may have been, was a lie. While he was imprisoned, Junius wrote a letter to his daughter describing all that he had endured.[3] This letter, heartbreaking as it is to read, shines important light on how confessions such as this one were forced out of accused witches.

> Many hundred thousand times good night, my daughter Veronica so dear to my heart. Innocent I came to jail, innocent I was tortured, innocent I must die.
>
> . . . When the executioner took me back to jail, he said to me: 'Sir, I beg you, for God's sake confess something, whether it be true or not. Invent something, for you cannot bear the torture which you shall suffer; and even if you bear it all, you still shall not escape, not even if you were a count, but one torture will follow another until you say you are a witch. Not before that will they let you go, as you may see by their trials, for one is just like another.'

Heal the Witch Wound

... Now dear child, here you have all my confession and [the record of] my trial, for which I must die. And they are sheer lies and inventions, so help me God. For I was forced to say all this through fear of the torture that was threatened beyond what I had already endured. For they never leave off with the torture till one confesses something; no matter how pious he really is, he must be a witch.

... Good night, for your father Johannes Junius will never see you again.

Though the witch hunts impacted nearly every region of the European continent, it was Germany that became the epicenter and remained so for more than a hundred years. To truly put this in perspective, consider this staggering statistic: during the period with the highest number of witchcraft-related executions in Europe (1580–1630), an estimated 40 percent of deaths took place in the region that is modern-day Germany. What's more, three out of every four accused witches lived in what were German-speaking lands at the time.[4]

Why did the witch craze burn through Germany with such ferocity? One possible answer is the Protestant Reformation—a major religious movement that challenged the authority of the Catholic Church and birthed Protestantism. Germany was the starting point of the Reformation wave that swept first through the Holy Roman Empire and then the rest of Europe, which also meant it was a hotbed of religious conflict.

To defend the validity and honor of their respective denominations, clergy from both sides rushed to develop creeds and strict social standards to which their members would be held. When members defied these norms, they were punished harshly—after all, one ill-behaved Catholic or Protestant might reflect poorly upon the entire denomination. This religious warfare almost certainly contributed to the intense witch trial activity in Germany, as few misdeeds were as dangerous as witchcraft in the eyes of the clergy, the state, and society at large.[5]

Witch Trials Throughout Europe

News of the German witch trials spread far and wide, sparking witch-hunting hysteria across Europe. Switzerland and Austria trailed closely beyond Germany in terms of the number of persons tried and executed. Following these regions, France, Scotland, Denmark, Hungary, and Poland initiated some of the most bloodthirsty witch hunts in Europe.[6] Trials also occurred in England, Norway, Sweden, the Netherlands, Belgium, Ireland, Russia, Estonia, and elsewhere in Europe. Most of these are poorly documented, their stories and statistics clouded by the dust of time.

The French-speaking lands were home to the second-heaviest concentration of witch trials after the German-speaking lands, particularly northern France.[7] Though the true figures are unknown, an estimated 5,000 trials and 2,500 executions related to witchcraft occurred in the area of modern France, though many of these were at the time located within the borders of the Holy Roman Empire.[8] Most accusations were against the poorest members of the community and made by those who were better off or at least marginally so.

Beginning in 1542, England, Scotland, Wales, and Ireland passed a succession of Witchcraft Acts introducing severe punishments. Of these, Scotland oversaw the harshest persecution of witches: an estimated 4,000 individuals were tried for witchcraft in Scotland, culminating in 1,500 executions. Many trials were overseen by King James VI, who later went on to publish the summation of his experience persecuting witches in a series of books known as *Daemonologie*.

Sweden enacted its own Witchcraft Act in 1608, introducing the death penalty for all practitioners of magic. Over the next century an estimated four hundred individuals were executed for witchcraft in Sweden. Most of the deaths occurred during the eight-year period known as the Great Noise (1668–1676), which began when twelve-year-old Gertrud Svendsdotter accused twenty-five-year-old Märet Jonsdotter of bringing her to Blåkulla, the legendary isle of the Witches' Sabbath, to meet with the Devil. Märet maintained her innocence throughout the entirety of the trial—save for a handful of harmless folk magic practices, such as blessing salt to cure sick cows—until her execution in 1672. This narrative of witches indoctrinating children by transporting them to Blåkulla became a central theme in many of Sweden's trials.

One of the most well-known victims of the Scandinavian witch hunts was a Norwegian woman named Lisbet Nypan, who was tried alongside her husband Ole. Lisbet was a healer who had used folk charms to treat illnesses for over three decades. The townsfolk were suspicious that she had also been using baneful magic to cause illness, ensuring a market for her healing services. Both Lisbet and Ole were found guilty and executed.

And what of Southern Europe? Given the power of the Holy Inquisitions in Italy and Spain, it would be logical to assume the witch craze burned through the Mediterranean with the same ferocity as in Western and Northern Europe—yet this was not the case. Religious leaders in Spain, Italy, and Portugal largely viewed witchcraft as an act of wrong belief rather than diabolism and sought to punish and correct practitioners of magic rather than execute them.[9] Of those individuals who were prosecuted for witchcraft in Southern Europe, most were well-known diviners and healers—including priests who incorporated folk magic into their Christian healing methods.

The Wounds of the Past

Producing confessions was central to trying suspected witches. With a few exceptions, canon law prevented the accused from being executed if they maintained their innocence. Thus, torture was used liberally by witch-hunters. These methods relied on significant physical violence, often of a sexual nature.

In many cases, the interrogation of a suspected witch began with stripping her naked, shaving all her body hair, and searching the entirety of her body for a telltale witches' mark, usually in front of a crowd of witnesses. It was believed that these marks could be either visible or invisible. Those that were visible usually took the form of moles, warts, birthmarks, scars, skin tags, or wounds. These were thought to be witches' teats from which demons, imps, and animal familiars could suckle—a perversion of the nurturing reality of breastfeeding.

Invisible marks were identified via the prick test. During this invasive test, needles were repeatedly stuck into every part of the flesh to find areas that were insensitive to pain—a sign of the Devil's influence. These tests were occasionally successful, as the human body can become desensitized to pain after hours of physical torment, causing the person to become unresponsive to continued abuse. Additionally, some witch-hunters may have also used retractable needles and sleight of hand to ensure the success of the prick test.[10] Whether visible or invisible, these witches' marks were often found in the accused's mouth or genitals.

Most often, the suspected witch would maintain their innocence through the duration of the prick test. In this case, the next step was imprisonment. Unclothed, the accused would be forced to sit upon a stool in a cell for days without food, water, or sleep. In some instances, jailers forced them to walk back and forth repeatedly, without rest, until blisters or physical exhaustion caused them to collapse. This lack of sleep and nourishment caused both immense distress as well as delirium and was highly effective at producing wild confessions.

Cucking stools (also called ducking stools) were a type of chair attached to a free-moving beam upon which an individual could be bound and submerged in a body of water. These stools were used both as a means of punishment and interrogation, and later gave way to the swimming test, where a suspected witch was bound and dumped into a body of water. If she floated to the surface, she was a witch; if she sank, she was innocent. Those who sank were retrieved from the water, but drownings were nevertheless a common occurrence.

Other common methods of torture used during the Burning Times included the thumbscrew, the boot, the rack, and the strappado. One device that was almost entirely limited to use on female victims was the witch's bridle, also known as the scold's bridle. This device—an iron muzzle that enclosed the head and was outfitted with a bit that went into the mouth, often with a sharp spike that pressed down upon the tongue—was used to quite literally silence suspected witches. Attempting to speak while wearing the scold's bridle could tear the tongue, causing horrific pain and permanent damage. Women were sometimes paraded through town while wearing the bridle in a display of public humiliation.

Agnes Sampson, also known as the Wise Wife of Keith, was a Scottish healer and suspected witch who was tried and executed during Scotland's North Berwick witch trials. During her imprisonment she endured many of the methods of torture discussed above: she was stripped naked, her entire body and head were shaved, and she was searched for a witches' mark, which was found in her genitals. She was also subjected to sleep deprivation and forced to wear a witch's bridle, which was fastened to her cell wall. After confessing to the crimes for which she was accused, Agnes Sampson was strangled to death and burned as a witch.

At this point, I must warn you that I have reserved one of the most abhorrent tales for last. While the details of the Pappenheimer family trial in Munich in 1600 are difficult to stomach, their ordeal exemplifies the cruel, totalitarian nature of Europe's witch trials—how these accusations were used not just to punish individual "crimes," but as a weapon of inciting mass panic and asserting total control.[11] The Pappenheimers were a family of five who belonged to Germany's lowest socioeconomic class. After being accused of witchcraft, Anna Pappenheimer, her husband Paulus, and their two eldest sons were imprisoned and tortured. Under duress they recounted wild, graphic tales of having sexual intercourse with the Devil, blighting fields and harvests, summoning storms, and slaying hundreds of babies and children to make potions.

All four adult Pappenheimers were sentenced to death, while the youngest son—ten-year-old Hansel—was ordered to attend his family's execution. A crowd of over a thousand people gathered and watched as the Pappenheimers were stripped naked, tortured with red-hot tongs, and paraded through the city streets. When they reached the place of execution, the four Pappenheimers were tied to their respective stakes and burned alive. Hansel would be executed as well several months later.

It is no coincidence that this sadistic performance and others like it took places in front of crowds numbering in the thousands. What better way to keep the masses—particularly those who have reason to revolt against the ruling class—in their place than by subjecting them to the gruesome reality of what can happen to anyone who steps out of line? The hellish Pappenheimer trial was much more than the simple execution of four suspected witches—it was a warning. The messaging of these displays of violence was clear and direct: Seeking power while existing in a female body is dangerous. Defying societal norms around gender and sexuality is dangerous. Speaking out against injustice is dangerous. Questioning the authority of those in power is dangerous. Offending the wrong person is dangerous. Trusting in your friends and neighbors is dangerous. Believing in pagan superstitions is dangerous. Being different is dangerous—so keep to yourself, keep quiet, keep your head down, and keep out of the way.

The handful of tales highlighted in this chapter hardly scratch the surface of what is known about the European witch craze, much less what is still to be uncovered. Entire books have been dedicated to understanding this dark time in history, and even those devoted tomes do not touch on every trial, every murder, every village plagued by hysteria and violence. A conservative and largely agreed-upon estimate of the number of people executed during the Burning Times is 50,000, though other scholars have proposed the true figure is closer to 100,000 or more.[12] Many of the trials were poorly documented, and those that were recorded were clearly skewed by fear and religious fanaticism, clouding the truth of the situation.

Still, this curated collection of stories provides a meaningful glimpse into the horror of the Burning Times—a time when neighbor turned upon neighbor, sibling upon sibling, and child upon parent; a time when it was dangerous to be too poor or too wealthy, too unattractive or too beautiful, too anonymous or too celebrated; a time when practicing folk healing, offending the wrong person, or simply being in the wrong place at the wrong time could lead to imprisonment, torture, and death.

3

The Role of Gender in the Witch Trials

No crystal ball is needed to see that the witch craze was steeped in misogyny and contempt for women. Superstitious fervor no doubt played its role, but we can't overlook the fact that the witch hunts systematically targeted women as a means of diminishing their socioeconomic, sexual, and spiritual power.

And yet, an estimated ten thousand men were also executed during the Burning Times. If the witch craze was the by-product of misogyny and patriarchy, where do these men fit into the narrative? In this chapter we will explore the role of gender in the witch trials, as well as the interplay between gender and other key factors like capitalism, imperialism, ableism, and homophobia.

This focus on the two genders of male and female may seem narrow and antiquated to you; I agree wholeheartedly. The male-female binary leaves little room for nonbinary, gender-fluid, gender nonconforming, and other queer folks in this discussion. Unfortunately, we are bound to the views of the era we are discussing. Trial documents virtually never broach the topic of sexual orientation, much less gender identity or expression, which were not well understood in the early modern period.

While it is very possible that some of the victims of the Burning Times would identify outside of the gender binary if they were alive today, the lack of documentation means the only discussions we can have are purely speculative. Yet keeping in mind what we already know about the witch trials—that they were largely used to control and silence people who were "other" than those in power—it certainly seems likely that nonbinary and gender-fluid folks *would* have been targeted by the Church during this time. I believe it is important to hold space for this theory even as we narrow the scope of our discussion to women and men.

Women in the Burning Times

Of the fifty thousand or more people executed in Europe as witches, 80 percent were women. It is no coincidence that this mass persecution of women occurred alongside the rise of capitalism (the privatization of land), patriarchy (the restriction of women's sexuality and economic roles), and religious intolerance (as Catholic and Protestant clergy fought for authority and control). As Silvia Federici notes in *Witches, Witch-Hunting, and Women,* indicators of the true crimes of suspected witches lie in the accusations against them: casting baneful magic upon what had once been communal lands, bewitching the crops and livestock of landlords and those in power, promiscuous behavior, being quarrelsome and having evil tongues, begging on neighbors' doorsteps and cursing those who refused to help them, and otherwise rejecting their societal position as subordinate to men.[1]

Why were more women tried and executed for witchcraft than men? Because women—particularly elderly, impoverished women—were the primary victims as well as the primary opponents of the "restructuring of rural Europe at the dawn of capitalism."[2]

Within the system of capitalism, female bodies are resources to be exploited. In early modern Europe, this exploitation ensured the success of two goals: the creation of a large and powerful workforce and shifting women from working and earning income independently to a subservient role as wives and homemakers.[3] Again, the evidence lies in the accusations: "witches" were often accused of nothing more than promiscuity, adultery, abortion, or bearing illegitimate children. We see this theme appear again in the sexual nature of the torture used against suspected witches.

Yet perhaps most threatening of all to the ruling structures of early modern European society were the women who stood tall in their Divine Feminine power—those who practiced herbal healing, midwifery, divination, and folk magic that had been passed down from grandmothers to mothers to daughters for generations. These women commanded respect from their communities and used their intuitive wisdom and skills to earn a living, and that made them strong—and a threat to the systems of capitalism, patriarchy, and religion that were rising to new levels of power and control. What's more, many of these women were the same ones participating in enclosure riots and demanding a return to a more communal way of living—an echo of pagan times, when communities shared the bounty of the harvest and the hunt in the form of seasonal feasts.

Indeed, we see again and again how disdain for the old pagan ways played a role in the witch hunts. Pre-Christian societies viewed women as the "weavers of memory" who passed down folkloric wisdom from mother to daughter and who kept old customs and traditions alive through the art of oral storytelling.[4] These memories of pagan values ran the risk of empowering laborers and disempowering those who would exploit them. Thus, in the sixteenth century a full-out war was waged against the last remnants of this older way of being—and against women's voices. The witch hunts resulted in the destruction of not only tens of thousands of women, but also of feminine knowledge passed down through generations.

Of course, witch-hunting propaganda did not lay out these motives in such plain terms. The *Malleus Maleficarum* did not condemn women for threatening capitalism or the status of men as superior to women. Instead, it condemned them for being inherently wicked, defective, intellectually inferior, deceitful, and sexually depraved. There was no need to further explain why it was wrong for a woman to have too much power, as these accusations preemptively shut down every possible defense. This was the core psychology behind the misogyny of the Burning Times.

Men in the Burning Times

While the witch hunts were largely a targeted attack on women, we would be remiss to ignore that an estimated 20 percent of all victims of the witch hunts were men. Although male witches were an anomaly in regions such as Germany, in others men were persecuted at equivalent or higher rates compared to women. These regions include Finland, Estonia, Iceland, Russia, Burgundy, and Normandy, where sorcery and magic were more commonly associated with men. Of the 641 people accused of sorcery in Finland, 49 percent were men.[5] Most were elderly healers and wise men who were suspected of using baneful magic to harm livestock and poison food.

In rural Normandy, the majority of individuals persecuted for witchcraft were male shepherds. Unlike the women accused of witchcraft in other French regions, these "shepherd-witches" were not charged with inflicting malicious magic upon their neighbors. Rather, they were suspected of using magical charms to protect their livestock or to harm the livestock of other shepherds. The creation of these charms was believed to involve stealing the Eucharist from churches, which was the true crime in the eyes of the Church. Between 1590 and 1635, over sixty shepherds were tried for witchcraft by the Parliament of Rouen, and at least twenty were executed.[6]

In Estonia and Iceland, the witch craze largely centered around converting Indigenous populations to Christianity. Paganism and folk magic traditions remained strong in these rural regions, especially among the working class, and accusations of witchcraft typically excluded the satanic rhetoric that was central to trials in the German lands. Respectively, 60 percent of the 200 people in Estonia and 90 percent of the 120 people in Iceland prosecuted for witchcraft were men.[7] While magic was seen as a feminine art in pre-Christian Nordic society, this viewpoint shifted during the Middle Ages. By the start of the Burning Times, Icelandic magic was primarily practiced by men. As a result, of the twenty-two individuals executed for sorcery in Iceland, just two were women.

Though most of Austria's witch trials did in fact target women, one stands in stark contrast: the Zaubererjackl witch trials, which spanned the years 1675–90 in Salzburg. Over two hundred individuals were accused of working under the guidance of a mysterious wizard known as Jäckel, almost all of them homeless boys and men younger than twenty-two. As rumors of this shrouded figure swept through Salzburg, fantasy melded with fact and gave rise to moral hysteria. Jäckel was said to wear a magical coat that helped him disappear from sight, aiding him in violent murders and other crimes. He was also said to convert gangs of beggar children and teenagers to his dark ways through baneful magic and sodomy.

While the spectral Jäckel was never apprehended, scores of homeless youths were locked in cells, interrogated, and tortured. Most were found guilty and executed through burning, hanging, or decapitation. Ultimately, 139 lives were claimed—70 percent of them male, 70 percent younger than twenty-two years old, and all but two beggars.[8] No doubt this population was targeted and vilified because they reminded Salzburg's citizens of a much more real, yet more abstract threat: that of looming poverty, socioeconomic inequality, and hunger.

Lastly, we cannot overlook the role of homophobia in accusations of witchcraft, especially against men. Regardless of gender, witches were believed to be sexually insatiable and guilty of fornicating with the Devil himself. For men, this carried the weight of a second accusation: sodomy, which was viewed as a serious moral crime punishable by mutilation and death. Sodomy was not typically presented as the primary offense, but was leveraged to further malign the accused and weaken their ability to defend themselves.

Given what we know about the role of gender in the witch trials, it may not be surprising to learn that in modern times, the concept of the witch wound often resonates most strongly for women—so much so that the witch wound is considered by many to be a "feminine wound." Indeed, in educating about this work online, I have received thousands of comments and messages from women who carry the witch wound and are doing the work to heal themselves.

And yet, I have also heard from men and nonbinary folks who have been deeply impacted by the witch wound. Considering that one in every five victims of the Burning Times were men and that there are modern-day witches and spiritual seekers of all genders, this isn't surprising. While it would be wrong to ignore the fact that the witch trials were largely a targeted attack on women and women's bodies—and that these attacks are still ongoing today—it would likewise be wrong to deny people of other genders their right to claim this healing work.

My personal belief is that while the witch wound can express as a feminine wound, it can also express as an otherness wound. Additionally, an individual's gender may impact how they personally experience the witch wound—just as gender influenced how and why people were targeted during the Burning Times.

4

The Legacy of the Witch Craze

In learning about the history of the witch trials, there is one question many modern witches and spiritual practitioners want answered: how many of the individuals persecuted for witchcraft during the Burning Times were *actually* witches? Historians cannot seem to agree—after all, most modern scholars do not believe in magic to begin with—nor can contemporary witches. As in most disagreements, the truth no doubt lies somewhere between all and none. Scholarly research indicates that most witchcraft accusations were used as weapons by those in power to inflict terror and control over the greater population. While those accused may have been guilty of other infractions—like having a female body and/ or threatening the foundations of inequality—witchcraft was *usually* not one of them.

However, we also know various forms of magic have existed as extensions of human spirituality and culture since antiquity. As in every era that preceded it, early modern Europe was drenched in magic and superstition. *Popular magic* is the name given to the customs and traditions of the common people: packing herbs into protective amulets while reciting prayers and incantations, burying objects with special significance around the property to protect livestock and bring good fortune, drawing sigils or planting certain herbs in front of the home to ward off malicious spirits.

In these times, magical experts provided additional services that were above the skill level of the common folk, just as they have since the dawn of civilization. These individuals have been called by many names through the ages: high priests and priestesses, oracles, druids, hierophants, and shamans. In pre-Christian societies they often served as political advisors. While their influence had declined by the Middle Ages, these seers and diviners remained highly valued members of their communities well into the early modern era. Townsfolk turned to such mages for all manner of services: healing the sick, finding stolen or lost goods, predicting the future, concocting love potions, protecting crops and livestock, expelling baneful spirits and summoning helpful ones, and banishing misfortune from towns and villages.

Understandings of magic, religion, science, and medicine were woven together into holistic practices that would seem wildly out of place in today's world, but were run-of-the-mill in early modern Europe. Even priests and doctors dabbled in practices such as performing divination and reciting incantations at certain times of the day to cure illnesses. The Renaissance gave rise to a renewed interest in hermeticism, alchemy, astronomy/astrology, and ceremonial magic, though these were primarily practiced by the educated elite.

Given the scale of the European witch craze, it seems statistically likely that some of its victims had knowledge of magical practices such as those outlined in the paragraphs above, even if these practitioners likely would have rejected the label *witch*. How large a group was this? Unfortunately, this is a truth that has been lost to time and unlikely to be recovered.

Yet in the context of tending the witch wound, the unknowable reality of this dark time in history *does not actually matter*. Witches or not, tens of thousands of innocent humans were imprisoned, tortured, and brutally murdered because of the mere *perception* that they were witches—that they had the power to inflict their will upon the world by harnessing unseen forces. *That* is the true essence of the witch wound: the collective memory that countless individuals were exiled from their communities and killed in the most barbaric of ways because of the terror and outrage invoked by the very *idea* of magic and witchcraft.

This memory lives on in our collective unconscious and in our blood and bones, having been passed down to us to through the witches and cunning folks who survived the Burning Times, through the horrified crowds of onlookers who witnessed their neighbors and friends being burned alive, and even through the witch-hunters and executioners themselves. Regardless of who our ancestors were or who we ourselves may have been in past lifetimes, there is no escaping the scars that remind us of a time when magic was feared and punished and when those who practiced it were regarded as the epitome of evil and danger.

This is the wound that makes it feel unsafe to proclaim our truths, to boldly live in our magic, to share our gifts with the world, and to trust in the wisdom of our bodies. This is the wound that makes us doubt our powers and hide our true natures out of shame and guilt. This is the wound that makes us mistrust those around us—especially women, because our psyches remember a time when female friendships were threatening and unsafe.

Some modern witches have clear memories of being persecuted for witchcraft in past lifetimes, while others have traced their lineages back to historical witches or victims of the Burning Times. Yet neither is required to feel the pain of the witch wound, because this wound is kept alive *by society itself*. It affects all people who are different or other from the people in power—people who are not Christian, male, white, able-bodied, and heteronormative and people who dare to break free of societal expectations—whether they claim the title witch or not. Above all else, the witch trials taught people to conform or risk pain and death. That wound is deep, painful, and real.

There is a saying in many esoteric communities: "As above, so below; as within, so without; as the universe, so the soul." One interpretation of this phrase is that everything that happens on the mundane, material plane is reflected in the spiritual plane and vice versa. I believe this is an apt way of understanding the witch wound. We find healing medicine in the study of both the magical and mundane causes of this wound: the persecution of folks who practiced witchcraft and used their power to influence the world around them and the systemic oppression of women, normalization of violence against the other, and prosecution of anyone daring to speak against injustice, patriarchy, capitalism, colonialism, and religious tyranny. Similarly, by understanding the witch wound on both a personal, spiritual level and a global, cultural scale, we can facilitate deeper healing.

The Echo of the Witch Craze Through Time and Space

The impact of early modern Europe's witch hunts reverberated through both time and space. It wasn't long before panic and hysteria traveled across the Atlantic to the shores of North America. Between February 1692 and March 1693, over two hundred people were accused of witchcraft in the town of Salem, Massachusetts. Thirty were found guilty, and twenty were executed.

Just as the mass hysteria of the Burning Times spread to the North American colonies, it also found its way to other regions impacted by European colonialism and imperialism . . . which, of course, is most of the planet. People are often shocked to learn that the witch trials didn't end with Salem, but are in fact still taking place around the globe. As Silvia Federici explains in *Witches, Witch-Hunting, and Women*, this globalization of violence against women and suspected witches was—and continues to be—primarily driven by capitalist development.[1] Recall how the European witch craze coincided with the rise of capitalism, patriarchy, and religious reformation. Just as the trials in Europe were a thinly veiled attempt to restrict women's bodily and economic autonomy and to silence those who spoke out against wealth inequality and the privatization of land, so are today's trials in India, Nepal, Tanzania, Kenya, Ghana, Papua New Guinea, and Saudi Arabia.

In India, an estimated two hundred women are executed for witchcraft every year. These women are often widows or divorcées who own land or other resources. In Papua New Guinea, a Sorcery Act—not unlike those of the Burning Times—was in effect until 2013. Even though this act has been repealed, witch hunts in Papua New Guinea have continued to increase rapidly over the past decade. In this nation of eight million, upward of two hundred people—usually elderly women or individuals who are mentally or physically ill—are murdered for the crime of witchcraft every year.[2] And the African continent has experienced some of the most brutal witch hunts not just in modern times, but in all of history—even compared to Europe's Burning Times. Between 1991 and 2001, an estimated 23,000 individuals were executed for witchcraft in Africa.[3] This is a conservative estimate; some experts believe the number of executions may be nearly double that figure. Tanzania, Ghana, Gambia, Sierra Leone, Cameroon, and the Democratic Republic of the Congo are among the nations that have been particularly afflicted. Again, we see striking similarities between what is happening in Africa today and what occurred in Europe over three hundred years ago. Today's witchcraft accusations in Africa often center around themes of cannibalism, causing illness and sterility, and destruction of crops and personal property. Furthermore, the accused are usually elderly women who live alone on their own land, while their accusers are often younger, male members of their communities.[4]

But we do not have to look to Africa or the South Pacific to understand the long-lasting impacts of the witch craze; the Western world has plenty of its own modern-day holdovers to navigate. In the 1980s, a moral panic known as the satanic panic spread like wildfire throughout the United States. Over the next decade, more than ten thousand accusations of satanic ritual abuse were launched nationwide.[5] The claim: that Devil-worshipping cult members were performing bizarre occult rituals involving the physical and sexual abuse of children. Sightings of witches, sometimes flying on brooms, were featured in multiple cases. Even the role-playing game Dungeons & Dragons came under fire from religious fundamentalists arguing that it promoted witchcraft and satanism.

Thousands of individuals were accused of cult involvement and dozens wrongfully convicted on charges of child abuse, often on the basis of nothing more than their hobbies, interests, and clothing choices. Many of the accused were teachers and day care staff; others were teenagers who listened to heavy metal and embraced goth fashion. While most of these convictions were later overturned due to lack of evidence, dozens of innocent people spent years—in some cases, decades—of their lives in prison for crimes they did not commit.[6] There is no doubt that this was a challenging and unsafe time for witches, as well as those who followed Earth-based and New Age religions.

Satanic cults, baneful magic, child abuse, sexual depravity . . . if these claims sound eerily familiar, that's because you have heard them all before. Not only do they mirror the accusations launched against suspected witches during the Burning Times, but these statements continue to be used to defame and discredit individuals today. While it is often said that the satanic panic died out in the 1990s, the truth is that it is still very much a part of our modern culture.

Today, countless individuals remain swept up in the same fear of magic and the occult that has plagued our society for centuries. Much like in the Burning Times, these accusations of evil magic and Devil worship are sometimes used as weapons against specific individuals—often those who are outspoken or too other—and other times are born out of pure collective fear and hysteria. As recently as 2022, American churches have made the news for throwing Ouija boards, tarot cards, and Harry Potter books into bonfires.[7] As the German writer Heinrich Heine famously said, "Where they burn books, they will also ultimately burn people."

Is it a coincidence that we are currently being affected by the same global challenges that plagued Europe during the Burning Times,

Heal the Witch Wound

including wealth inequality, political hostility, climate change, and disease? I don't believe it is. While much has changed since the first witch burning, one thing has certainly remained the same: as humans, it is in our nature to seek scapegoats for what we do not understand or cannot bear to face.

Once again—and not for the first time—history is repeating itself. Is it any wonder that the impact of the Burning Times can still be felt so viscerally by modern practitioners of magic, esotericism, and spirituality, as well as by women, people of color, people with disabilities, members of the LGBTQ+ community, and all who are not represented by those in power?

Of course, we cannot forget that patriarchy, imperialism, capitalism, and religious intolerance are still major forces in our modern-day society—just as they were during the Burning Times. The midwives and herbalists who were persecuted for providing abortions and other reproductive care in the early modern period would no doubt be disheartened to learn that these same rights are still being threatened by government leaders today, just as the individuals who were persecuted for begging and protesting would be dismayed to learn that our modern society is not much kinder to those in need than the one they lived in.

Misogyny, patriarchy, toxic masculinity, colonialism, imperialism, racism, antisemitism, ableism, religious intolerance, greed, moral panic, oppression—these are the ingredients that simmer in the cauldron of the witch wound. They are also the answer to the question of why the witch wound is so insidious: because they plague our modern society and culture just as they plagued the European continent during the Burning Times. Today's witch hunts and conspiracy theories are no different from those of the past. They function as diversions from the true evil: all forms of inequality and systemic oppression.

Healing the witch wound is not a fast or easy process, but understanding how it came to exist is an important first step. Dissecting the complex history of the witch hunts also demonstrates exactly why this healing work is so necessary: just as the witch wound itself has reverberated through time and space, so can the healing medicine. When we heal the witch wound in ourselves, we also help to heal the collective, to create a better world for future generations, and to honor those who were so wrongfully persecuted during the Burning Times.

Part Two

SYMPTOMS OF THE WITCH WOUND

At the start of part one, I asked you to begin this healing journey by inhaling deeply and exhaling completely, allowing your body and mind to settle before diving into the deep and heavy work we have just completed. As we leave behind the horrors of the past and prepare to venture into the next stage of our journey together, I invite you to do the same now: inhale deeply—pause, allowing yourself to feel the magic and potential of this liminal space—then exhale deeply and slowly. Let your awareness anchor you into this present moment, readying you for the next phase of healing.

Likewise, I asked you at the start of part one to become the master of your own healing journey by noticing which sensations and emotions bubbled to the surface as you learned about the tragedies and atrocities of the Burning Times. You may have experienced visceral feelings of grief, rage, horror, anxiety, or disgust as you worked your way through the previous chapters. Perhaps these stories reminded you of certain experiences from your own lifetime—this one, or even a previous lifetime you cannot quite remember.

These sensations are precious gifts from your body and your highest self, pointing you in the direction of what most needs to be healed. In the subsequent chapters we will explore the ways the witch wound most commonly manifests: hiding your spiritual gifts and abilities, muting your self-expression, feeling stuck or blocked, ancestral wounding, past-life memories, strange physical sensations and fears, and a damaged relationship with the Divine Feminine, among others. Allow your intuitive somatic and emotional responses to guide you through this work.

You may discover that all of these signs and symptoms resonate for you, or you may find that some do while others do not. In either case, hold space for the wisdom of your body and trust in what is coming up for *you*. I am here to guide and support you, but ultimately, this is your journey. Grant yourself the freedom to wander and explore your own unique thoughts, memories, experiences, fears, and hopes. Know that you are held and validated by the countless individuals who are working to heal this same wound, but also know that you are free to draw your own conclusions.

Are you ready? Let's move forward into the next phase together.

Hiding in the
Spiritual Broom Closet

Have you ever hidden your spiritual beliefs and magical practices from others out of fear of being judged, ridiculed, or rejected? Feelings of fear and shame about practicing magic live at the very heart of the witch wound. It is not difficult to understand why: for a period spanning multiple centuries, suspected practitioners of the magical arts were vilified, demonized, and persecuted. An all-out war was waged against the remnants of Europe's pagan history that had been preserved and passed down through folk customs and superstitions for generations.

Cunning folk who crafted herbal remedies and protective amulets were labeled charlatans. Midwives were blamed for infant deaths and suspected of killing babes to feast upon them as a source of magical power. Acts as innocuous as preparing a healing charm for a sick cow or using divination to predict the weather could ignite the wrath of the witch-hunters. Even in modern times, the word *witch* conjures the image of an ugly old crone, cackling wickedly as she stirs her toxic brew.

Over time, this view of magic and witchcraft permeated our collective unconscious and our global culture. While the number of witches in the world is rising rapidly, we are still far outnumbered by nonwitches—

many harboring these antiquated views of magic. Though practicing witchcraft is no longer recognized as a legally punishable crime in the Western world, there are still some who would judge, shame, mock, ostracize, and even harm those of us who claim our magical birthrights and identify as witches.

At some level, all witches carry the memory of being exiled, tortured, and mutilated by members of their community for performing their craft and living in their power. It does not matter whether you were a witch in a past lifetime or one of your ancestors was involved in the witch trials. We *know* these atrocities were inflicted upon countless individuals, and we *know* the people who lived through these experiences played a role in shaping the world we now inhabit.

Of course this spiritual wound lives on in modern witches, healers, diviners, herbalists, and other magical practitioners. How could it not? This is why sharing your magic with others—even your partner, closest friends, and family members—can feel deeply threatening and unsafe. You might worry that if you open up about your beliefs and practices, you will be judged, mocked, or labeled as wicked, evil, crazy, dangerous, childish, silly, weird, or strange.

As a result, many witches make the choice to remain hidden "in the broom closet." This can present in downplaying your spiritual and magical practices to others, clearing off altars and putting away your magical tools and books when guests come to visit, and not wearing witchy jewelry or clothing out of the house. It can also manifest as a deep fear of sharing your magical and spiritual abilities; feelings of doubt, shame, and guilt about these gifts; and even the belief that magic and Earth-based spirituality are inherently harmful or dangerous.

Watering Down Your Magic

In my heart and soul, I have always been a witch and a pagan. I was born with a curious mind, a fascination with magic, a desire to help others, and a deep connection to the natural world around me. Yet for years, I refused to claim these titles. The tender, throbbing pain of the witch wound reminded me that once upon a time, baring my soul's truth to the world would have been wildly unsafe—and that in many ways, it still is today.

Over the years, as my practice sank deeper into the depths of the occult, my wounded inner witch begged and pleaded for me to veil these parts of myself—to enjoy them only in the safety of seclusion. During the first years of my practice, I had nightmares about accidentally outing myself as a witch to my wider social circle. It was hard to imagine anything worse than the people around me thinking I was some kind of freak, or worse—*crazy*. Those feelings of fear, shame, and embarrassment haunted me in my waking hours and persuaded me to stay silent.

So I watered down the way I spoke about my magic. While my inner world was steeped in esoteric learnings, powerful rituals, and time-honored ancestral traditions, I cast a spell of invisibility over these practices to the world around me. Though I deeply yearned to be seen and accepted for who I truly was, fear of judgment and rejection persuaded me to hide my magical abilities and knowledge from the world. Dimming my own light felt safer and more comfortable than letting it shine openly.

For years I shared only the bits and pieces of my spiritual practice that I knew were generally tolerated by the world at large, ever mindful of where that unspoken line between acceptable and unacceptable spiritual self-expression lay. To speak of manifesting my dreams was perfectly fine in many circles—perhaps even inspiring to some. To call this same practice casting a spell would bring sidelong glances and hushed judgy whispers. To call myself spiritual was something many people could relate to, but to call myself a witch? I knew the vast majority of the people around me would never understand.

While I spent my nights swaying beneath the full moon to the sound of drums, reciting prayers to old pagan gods and goddesses, casting protective circles, dressing candles with oils and herbs, crafting talismans and charms, studying runes, trance journeying to unseen realms, and birthing my will into the world through the magic of the spoken word, by day I referred to all these practices and more simply as meditation.

In the privacy of my own home, I built a beautiful altar space where I could practice my craft. I decorated it with all the magical symbols and tools I use for devotional acts and magical workings: pentagrams, crystals, candles, jars of herbs, a cauldron, a ritual rattle, runes and oracle cards, photos of my ancestors, statues of my gods and goddesses. My altar is my sacred space, my safe space. Yet for too long, I disassembled it whenever friends or family visited.

Perhaps you can relate. Perhaps you have been hiding your magic in the same way for months or years, in which case you would not find the revelation in the last paragraph particularly shocking. But I ask you to sit with the meaning of this confession for a moment: my fear of being seen in my magic was so strong that I willingly *disassembled my safe space in my own home* rather than out myself as a pagan and a witch to the people who love me most.

This is what it means to water down your magic—to disenchant your practices to make them more palatable for everyone but you; to hide the parts of yourself that make you feel comfortable, happy, and powerful for the benefit of others. Watering down your magic may help you avoid uncomfortable conversations with judgmental people in the short term, but in the long term it reinforces the belief that how other people perceive you is more important than how you perceive yourself.

This is a form of dimming your own light before anyone else can do it for you. By living small, we show the world it has nothing to fear from us. It is a promise to not become too loud, too bold, too powerful—after all, these were the very qualities that could spark the fury of the witch-hunters in the Burning Times.

Fear of Sharing Your Gifts

During the European witch craze, healers, herbalists, diviners, cunning folks, and other practitioners of magic were persecuted—exiled, tortured, and murdered—for sharing their gifts with the world. Many of these individuals had lived as cherished and important members of their communities for decades. But when illnesses, storms, famines, and other sudden misfortunes struck, they were made scapegoats.

This shift was no accident. The greedy, corrupt individuals who drove the forces of capitalism and patriarchy felt threatened by the power these wise folks wielded. The beloved village midwife competed for the same coin as the educated male doctor; the diviner threatened the authority of local religious leaders. Perhaps these men knew their words were filled with fraud, or maybe they believed their own lies. In any case, they sought to defame those who practiced magic by reminding the populace that those who could heal by magic could also harm by magic—and their smear campaigns were highly effective.

If you carry the witch wound, you may have even come to fear your own magic and all that makes you unique, to mistrust your gifts, to believe that you are a fraud, an imposter, unworthy. For hundreds of years, practitioners of magic were told exactly that—that their methods of healing were evil or inferior, that their voices were insignificant, and that their claims to power and influence were fraudulent and rooted in sin. All of us are programmed with centuries' worth of societal conditioning that tells us our innate psychic gifts are not to be trusted and emotions and intuition have no place in rational decision-making.

Have you ever had a strong intuition about a person or situation, but chose to ignore that feeling because you doubted yourself or didn't want to cause a scene? Have you ever created something you were proud of, but hesitated to share it because you were worried about how other people would react? Have you ever performed a magical working that yielded powerful results, but kept it to yourself to avoid being criticized or mocked?

No matter your skills and gifts—spellcasting, clairvoyance, divination, trance journeying, energy healing, herbalism—you deserve to feel safe in sharing them if you so choose. Of course, you are in no way obligated to share your gifts with anyone; they are yours to enjoy as you please. But if dreams of sharing your abilities and talents with the world burn bright within you, it would be a shame to let fear smother those flames. If and when these concerns do arise, acknowledge that they come from a place of self-preservation, but know you are not beholden to them.

What's more, if you offer your spiritual abilities as a service to others, you deserve you be paid a fair amount of money for them. *Money*—it's a dirty word in many spiritual circles, and again this mindset harks back to the Burning Times. Herbalists and midwives were criticized and chased out of their vocations by professionally trained doctors and priests.[1] Though these Earth-based healers had effectively treated illnesses, delivered healthy babies, and eased pain in their communities for decades, they were labeled witches and accused of using their powers to cause illnesses rather than cure them.

The impact of these accusations reverberates into our modern era. To accuse a professional witch or spiritual healer of selling snake oil is an incredibly harmful and defamatory charge. While there *are* fraudulent and unethical practitioners in the magical community—and it's important to be vigilant about potential red flags—many legitimate tarot readers, energy healers, herbalists, and psychics live in fear of these accusations, if only on a subconscious level. As a result, many of them severely undervalue and undercharge for their services. After all, ensuring your spiritual business never earns much money is an effective—albeit self-sabotaging—way to be certain you won't draw too much attention from those in power.

Belief That Magic Is Dangerous

In the Burning Times, witch-hunters used propaganda like the *Malleus Maleficarum* to generate widespread hysteria and panic. The gruesome details printed in the pages of this witch-hunting handbook spread like wildfire across the continent: that witches were sexually insatiable, driven by carnal lust to perform unspeakable sexual acts with the Devil, and that witches gained their magical powers by stealing newborn infants from their cribs and drinking their blood or cooking their body parts in cauldrons.

The truth is that witch has been a dirty word since the earliest recorded histories and has only been reclaimed within the last century. In no uncertain terms, the *Malleus Maleficarum* states: "The evils which are perpetrated by modern witches exceed all other sin which God has ever permitted to be done."[2] Is it any wonder that witchcraft still carries such immense stigma, or that so many people view magic as something inherently dangerous, rather than something that is our Earth-given right?

It's worth pointing out that there is a substantial difference between approaching magic with a healthy level of respect and caution—especially when you are still learning—and having strong emotional reactions of fear and aversion. In my own life, this wound has manifested as a deep mistrust of herbal healing. For years, I longed to experience the benefits of working with the plant allies that I had read about in so many books. Yet in practice, I felt a surge of anxiety anytime I steeped a simple cup of herbal tea.

Through societal conditioning, I had come to believe that traditional, Earth-based healing practices such as herbalism were not to be trusted. I also believed that herbs, plants, and all things harvested from nature were dirty and wild in a way that made them unpredictable, uncontrollable, and dangerous. As I became aware of how this fear was affecting my life, I made a conscious effort to overcome it by consuming a handful of beginner-friendly herbs on a regular basis: holy basil, lemon balm, valerian, turmeric. It took me weeks to overcome the worst-case scenario fears that swirled through my mind: visions of overdosing or having a bad reaction, despite the fact that these herbs are well-researched even by Western medical standards.

I have witnessed this same type of deeply ingrained fear of various spiritual and magical practices show up for countless other witches, especially among new practitioners seeking advice from more experienced witches online. Common concerns include the idea that even the simplest of spells, such as lighting a candle for protection, will draw the attention of demons and malicious entities. While it is true that spirits of all kinds are attracted to the energy generated by magic, beginner witches usually have very little to fear—especially if they are following energetic best practices like casting some form of protection and cleansing after spellwork.

At its core, witchcraft is not an inherently dangerous practice—at least no more so than driving, swimming, hiking, or all the other activities millions of people participate in every day, all of which come with their own risks and deserve to be approached with a healthy level of caution—just like practicing magic. The witch wound warps the true danger of witchcraft into something much more immediate and threatening, even to the point of scaring off interested practitioners from the craft.

In the earlier years of my practice, it was initially a relief to learn that I was not alone—that countless witches and spiritual individuals of all nationalities, ages, genders, and backgrounds were choosing to keep their practices hidden in the broom closet, because that secretive existence felt safer than being authentically seen. Yet the weight of this knowledge also made my heart ache. How many *millions* of us were out there feeling entirely alone and misunderstood, asleep to the reality that if we all allowed ourselves to be seen, there would be no reason to feel alone anymore?

This heartache turned to rage, and that rage solidified into an actionable thought: what if allowing myself to be truly seen helped me find and connect with those like-minded souls of the world? Would that not be worth the risk of judgment from those who are committed to misunderstanding and rejecting the real me? As I played with this thought, a small spark of hope ignited in my soul. Yet as is the case in any journey or rite of passage, thoughts and hopes are easy; making the first move often proves to be much more challenging. Those of us who wish to connect with our wild, magical roots and claim the title of witch must dig deep to recover what was lost during the Christianization of Europe and again during the Burning Times. In doing so, we disturb and disrupt the foundation upon which modern society was built. Without fail, this action will ruffle feathers and draw criticism from those whose power rests upon that corrupt bedrock.

In keeping with a centuries-old tradition, modern witches are judged, mocked, ostracized, and called names: weird, childish, silly, crazy, deranged, unstable, dangerous, sinful, wicked, Devil worshipper. Of course it feels safer to stay hidden within the spiritual closet when these are the accusations hurled at us. This backlash triggers the witch wound, awakening memories of being hunted by sadistic men and frenzied mobs, of being accused of murdering and feasting upon newborn babies, of being betrayed by our neighbors, friends, children, and partners.

If you have a habit of watering down your magic, dimming your own light, and downplaying your spiritual interests, abilities, and accomplishments, this may be your witch wound trying to keep you safe. And indeed, in an age where tolerance has worn thin and insult-slinging has become sport, it can feel more bearable to be accepted for who you aren't than rejected for who you are—for a time, anyway.

The Witch Wound Can Show Up As . . .

- Hiding your magical practices and interests in the broom closet

- Feelings of fear, shame, and guilt about your magical and spiritual beliefs

- Downplaying your practices to others

- Fear of being viewed as sinful, evil, crazy, dangerous, silly, or weird

- Hiding your altar, spiritual tools, jewelry, books, and tattoos

- Feelings of being an imposter, fraud, or unworthy of your spiritual gifts
- Discomfort about charging money for your spiritual services and goods
- Internalized belief that your version of spirituality and magic is dangerous or wrong

6

Muting Your
Self-Expression

Of all the ways the witch wound can show up, fear of being authentically heard and seen is undoubtedly the most pervasive. How often do you stifle your own voice out of fear of being too outspoken, too opinionated, too sensitive, too demanding, too honest, too much? On the opposite side of this binary, many of us stay silent because we carry the weight of feeling like we are not enough—not creative enough, not educated enough, not confident enough, not talented enough. Both limiting beliefs fester beneath the surface of the witch wound, causing many witches and other spiritual people to hide their thoughts, ideas, talents, and gifts out of fear of judgment and rejection.

Women, in particular, have been tasked with walking the fine line between too much and not enough since antiquity. Be beautiful and likable, but not too confident; be feminine and nurturing, but not too emotional; be talented and educated, but not too powerful. Stray too far in either direction, and you risk upsetting the delicate balance of societal norms—and suffering the socioeconomic consequences.

Variations of this behavioral tightrope act are likewise enforced against people of color, immigrants, people with disabilities, individuals who are gay, bisexual, transgender, or nonbinary and anyone else who does not fit into the socially preferred mold of white, male, straight, cisgender, monotheistic, neurotypical, able-bodied, and wealthy. The importance of intersectionality cannot be overstated here; each person experiences unique levels of privilege and oppression that define how much slack and maneuvering room they are granted by society, making it easier or harder to fall across that line into too much or not enough.

Witches, of course, land outside society's rigid boundaries of self-expression in their own ways. In past eras, this separation was often literal as well as metaphorical. Many healers and herbalists lived on the outskirts of villages, outside the relative safety of civilization. Per the rules of our modern capitalist, patriarchal, Christianized society, witches are both too much—too unorthodox, too outlandish, too eccentric—and not enough—not conventional enough, not obedient enough, not predictable enough. While many witches privately exist outside these oppressive boundaries, doing so in the public eye—or even in sight of friends and family members—can be highly triggering to the wounded inner witch.

Those of us who identify as witches, healers, psychics, pagans, animists, and spiritual seekers often feel lonely and misunderstood. Even if you have the good fortune of being accepted for who you are by the people in your inner circle, there is a good chance you still feel that sense of separation. The innate knowledge that you are different from the norm—and that your uniqueness carries some level of threat, even if not the physical variety—lives on in your subconscious mind, where it can warp and damage your sense of self. Certainly, this feeling of not fitting in is made worse when you are actively rejected by those around you.

During the Burning Times, standing out and speaking up meant risking literal persecution: imprisonment, torture, sexual assault, and murder. The scars of this trauma run deep in our collective unconscious; they remind us that in the not-so-distant past, being marked as different ran the risk of physical harm and death. Even today, being too much or not enough for modern society can mean being ostracized, judged, and shamed. In this way, the witch wound is your psyche's way of trying to keep you safe. Your consciousness holds this warning because your ancestors' bodies carried it over the span of generations, passing it down to you.

Why is it so scary to be authentically heard and seen? Because in the most beautiful and wild and powerful of ways, *you are different.* You are different in all the ways that would have threatened those in power during the Burning Times and, indeed, in all the ways that continue to threaten those in power today. Your wounded inner witch knows this and would rather you stay silent and remain safe than risk persecution by sharing your truth and being noticed. This is why the truths that feel most authentic to you may also be the most difficult and scary to share with the world.

Fear of Speaking Your Truth

What does it mean to speak your truth? In essence, speaking your truth means remaining authentic in who you are in all situations and not twisting your words or hiding your true thoughts and feelings for the sake of someone else's approval. Setting and upholding clear boundaries, stating your desires and opinions, making your likes and dislikes known, and sharing your feelings are all part of speaking your truth.

When communicating with someone you genuinely trust, speaking your truth can feel like openness and expansion in the body. Imagine you have been withholding an important truth and are finally able to open your heart to a dear friend or loving relative. This sensation is often described as a weight off the shoulders; it allows you to sit up taller, to expand your lungs and breathe more deeply, and to relax the muscles of your face, arms, and torso. When you share your truth, you honor the wisdom of your body, mind, heart, and soul. This alignment creates a state of flow and a feeling of ease.

Yet your wounded inner witch remembers the pain of persecution, and this can make exposing your authentic truth feel unsafe—even in situations where there is no physical threat. When this happens, you end up betraying your truth by saying things that contradict what you genuinely think, feel, and desire. Feel into this experience for a moment: imagine yourself saying yes to a request when you would rather say no, remaining quiet when you disagree with someone about a topic that is important to you, or giving your approval to something you secretly dislike.

Where does this betrayal of your truth show up in your body? For many witches, including myself, it manifests as constriction in the throat, jaw, and chest. You might feel your shoulders tensing up toward your ears, your jaw clenching, and your throat tightening around heartfelt words left unspoken. Symptoms can also be subtler, like feelings of emptiness or numbness. These sensations are your body's way of communicating that your emotional and energetic boundaries have been violated. For many of us, they are our daily reality—the result of a lifetime of broken boundaries and buried truths.

When we say the things we think other people want to hear rather than what we actually feel to avoid conflict and to make our interactions with others feel safer, it is called *fawning*. You may be familiar with the three traditional trauma responses: fight, flight, and freeze. Fawning is a fourth, lesser-known trauma response that was first identified by therapist Pete Walker in his book *Complex PTSD: From Surviving to Thriving*. People who fawn often have a deep desire to keep the peace and to be validated by others.

Without thoroughly examining this behavior, it's easy to assume fawning and people-pleasing are simply ways of being considerate, kind, and helpful. But when the witch wound is driving these actions, what is really happening is that your wounded inner witch is attempting to find safety by making your words as nonthreatening as possible to the people around you. In truth, fawning is not actually about the other person's feelings at all. Rather, it is about your own inherited fear of rejection, conflict, and persecution. And while fawning may help you sidestep uncomfortable confrontations, it comes at a cost: when you fawn, you merge your wishes and beliefs with those of the people around you and lose your own needs and sense of self in the process.

Heal the Witch Wound

The twisted, infuriating reality is that society conditions all of us to allow these boundary violations, and even to facilitate and welcome them. We are taught to be civilized and agreeable above all else, including in environments where we feel uncomfortable, unsafe, sad, or angry. We are taught to position societal expectations over the wisdom of our own bodies—the deep, ancient, somatic wisdom that urges us to speak, sing, yell, cry, laugh, and otherwise allow our bodies and voices to process and express our emotions in the way they are meant to.

We can return to what we learned about the archetypal victim of the Burning Times in part one: the elderly, impoverished, outspoken woman who participated in enclosure riots and verbally cursed her wealthy neighbors when they turned her away from their doorsteps. Tens of thousands of women who fit this description were permanently silenced in the most horrific and violent of ways—all because they dared to speak their truths, to cause a scene, to unleash their righteous anger, to bare their emotions and opinions to the world. Let us not forget the method of punishment that was used to injure and shame these candid women as they awaited their executions: the tongue-slicing, voice-restricting scold's bridle.

We can also reflect on the tragic tale of Johannes Junius, the mayor of Bamberg, who wrote a letter to his daughter explaining his reasons for falsely confessing to being a witch before he was burned alive. Why did Johannes confess? Because he was told by the executioner that he would continue to be subjected to horrific forms of torture if he did not. In truth, Johannes was among the many executed for witchcraft who were *not* witches. Yet through the gruesome punishments of his time, he learned this truth was unsafe to speak. Death was the preferred alternative to further pain and suffering, so he chose to sacrifice his authentic truth and find peace in a lie.

This example may seem paradoxical: if Johannes was not truly a witch, is his experience relevant in the context of the witch wound? In my opinion, it absolutely is. Johannes was a victim of the Burning Times who learned to silence his authentic truth to save himself from imprisonment and torture—even if that salvation was found in death.

Regardless of whether they were witches or not, tens of thousands of women, men, and children endured similar experiences. You needn't believe in magic or witchcraft at all to recognize the wound this sort of trauma might leave on the collective psyche.

Fear of Being Seen

Related to the fear of speaking your truth is the fear of being authentically seen. The difference lies in the action: speaking your truth is about sharing your beliefs and emotions, setting boundaries, and stating your needs and desires. Being seen is about simply existing in your truth and allowing others to witness that without attempting to hide, diminish, or justify yourself. When we allow someone to truly see us, we invite a deeper, more authentic connection.

Being seen means allowing our raw, complex, multidimensional, messy, beautiful natures to shine forth—unfiltered, unedited, and unabridged. Of course, very few people are comfortable with this level of exposure and vulnerability. There is a reason speaking in front of a crowd is said to be more widely feared than death! Human beings are complicated creatures, yet society tells us it's not okay for us to display the full spectrum of who we are.

How many times over the course of your life have you swallowed your emotions rather than letting those around you bear witness to the unleashing of your truth? How many times have you berated your own body for needing to cry, laugh, or move in so-called inappropriate moments or situations? How many times have you denied both yourself and those around you the opportunity to authentically connect over heavy topics or deep truths?

Consider the reflex of crying. Generally speaking, it is not considered socially acceptable to cry in most public spaces or at social gatherings save for weddings and funerals. Yet at the same time, crying as an emotional response is the most natural thing in the world and something nearly every human can relate to and empathize with. Humans are social animals, and crying is an important reflex that signals our mood, feelings, and needs to the people around us. It also activates the parasympathetic nervous system, which allows us to self-soothe and stabilize our mood.

When we suppress this instinct out of fear of being seen as too sensitive, overly emotional, a downer, rude, or even unwell, we quite literally fight against our own body's means of regulating itself. We deny ourselves the opportunity to forge intimate, authentic connections and force ourselves to remain in an uncomfortable, isolated, dysregulated state—all because the fear of being seen in our raw, messy, complicated truth is too intense.

There are infinite scenarios in which a fear of being seen might cause you to hide your true nature from the people around you: the interests, hobbies, hopes, and dreams you discuss openly versus the ones you keep hidden; the clothes you choose to wear in various social situations; the photos you post on social media; the way you clean and rearrange your home before certain guests visit; and your struggles and victories with mental health.

When you edit your own self-expression out of a desire to fit in or meet the expectations of other people, you deny yourself the opportunity to be authentically seen. When someone bears the scars of the witch wound, this can feel particularly scary and threatening. During the Burning Times, being seen carried an even greater risk than judgment or rejection—it carried the risk of literal persecution, imprisonment, torture, and death. If the thought of being seen in all your magic, light, and power sends panic and dread through your body, it is very likely that your witch wound is being triggered.

Each time we silence our own truths or stifle our authentic self-expression, we betray ourselves. People-pleasing causes us to compromise our values, bottle our emotions, and neglect our needs. Dimming our own light damages our confidence and sense of self. Over time, this self-betrayal can lead to mental and emotional burnout, loss of identity, and feelings of bitterness and resentment. If your witch wound manifests in this way, you may often feel guilty, overstimulated, irritated, or angry without knowing why.

Every time you say yes when your heart screams no or shrink yourself to fit into the boxes assigned to you by society, you stoke the fire of resentment and rage that burns inside every wounded witch—a fire fueled by the heartbreak of self-betrayal and by the deeply ingrained memory of evil men who once built fires of their own to silence people like you.

Like all the natural elements, fire can serve as a tool for divine healing and creation, but only when it is properly controlled. Unbridled, fire represents chaos and destruction—and in most cases, the only person your inner rage-fire is burning is you. I know, because this was my story too. Before I could alchemize my fury into something healing and helpful, I first had to tame those wild flames by breaking the pattern of self-betrayal and self-silencing. Only then could I transmute my rage into passion, inspiration, and power.

With patience and grace, I invite you to make the first move here and now. Imagine you are in front of a crowd of your family, friends, acquaintances, coworkers, and neighbors. Imagine they are expectantly waiting for you to communicate with them. In this scenario, which truths feel impossible to convey? Which parts of yourself feel impossible to express? What do you imagine would happen if you expressed them anyway?

Imagine yourself sharing these forbidden truths boldly while surrounded by all the symbols and items that represent your most authentic self, proudly out in the open for all to experience. How does imagining this scene feel in your body? Does it feel threatening and unsafe? Does it feel freeing and exhilarating? There are no wrong answers. These instinctual responses are your body's way of showing where your witch wound lies. Explore these threads and follow them along your own individual path of healing.

As you embark on this journey, I give you this piece of wisdom to carry with you: the global population consists of nearly eight billion people who exist along an immense spectrum of cultural backgrounds, religious beliefs, moral philosophies, and other social constructs. Without fail, you will *always* be too much for many people and not enough for just as many. There is absolutely nothing you can do to be just right for everyone, but you can be just right for yourself. I hope this truth empowers you as it has empowered me.

The Witch Wound Can Show Up As . . .

- Stifling your self-expression

- Dimming your own light

- Silencing your own voice

- Minimizing your intuition and emotions

- Feelings of being too much or not enough

- Believing you can't fit in while being your authentic self

- Fawning, people-pleasing, and sharing only what you think others want you to

- Allowing your boundaries to be violated

- Feeling resentful, overstimulated, or angry without knowing why

7

Feeling Lost, Stuck, or Blocked

You were born with powerful magic within you. No different than the mountains, the seas, the forests, or the wild flora and fauna of Earth, you were born in sacred harmony and flow with the universe, with Source, with the Divine. Yet centuries of spiritual taming have stripped our society of this sense of interconnectedness, and as we grow up and are influenced by the modern world around us, we often lose sight of our own connections with the Divine. Though magic and nature-based spirituality are our sacred birthrights, they are pulled from our grasp before we even realize they are something that can be lost.

Through this process, an important component of the self is chipped away: that inner spark that guides us toward our dreams, our magic, and our most wild and powerful potential. Many spiritual, intuitive, creative people wander through life with the innate wisdom that they were born into this lifetime for an important reason—yet they feel blocked from fully accessing this deeper purpose. Indeed, this can be a manifestation of the witch wound: feeling ever burdened by the idea that there must be something *more* you should be doing with your time on Earth, while simultaneously feeling trapped in the same unfulfilling patterns and cycles.

You know you are here to make a difference—but what and how and when? It's like trying to remember the name of a song you loved years and years ago: You feel haunted by the ghost of its melody, but despite your best attempts, the lyrics—the crucial keys that will unlock that forgotten name—slip through your fingers like mist. So you drift along, sensing that something beautiful exists just outside the reaches of your memory, never quite knowing how to access it.

Feeling lost, stuck, or blocked is one of the less frequently discussed symptoms of the witch wound, yet I suspect it is one of the most common. You may feel as if you are not living up to your full potential—not necessarily in terms of income or career success, although this could certainly be one aspect of it—but in terms of something much deeper: your soul's purpose.

You might not know exactly what your purpose in this lifetime is supposed to be, but you have a gut feeling it is something that will leave a positive impact on the world around you. Perhaps you feel called to express yourself creatively, to stand against the injustices or evils of the world, to share your innate gifts and talents, or to help others in some way. You may simply feel drawn toward the idea of doing work that is deep and meaningful, even if you are not sure what form that work might take.

Despite this, you find yourself spinning your wheels and going nowhere. That vague sense of wanting to do something "more" feels far too big, too distant, too unreal. Instead, you search for ways to fit yourself into the more attainable, more clearly defined roles and identities outlined for you by society.

Even if you have a certain level of clarity regarding what your dream life looks like, you might choose to keep that dream tucked away in the back corners of your mind rather than exposing it to the light of the world. In doing so, you limit your own potential and stay safely within other people's expectations of you. This is your wounded inner witch trying to protect you by keeping you small.

Thus, the first step is to start thinking bigger. An important question to ask at this point in the journey is: Who are you? Who are you, *really?* Who are you outside the labels of partner, parent, child, sibling, friend, employee—all the roles that position you relative to another person? Who are you beyond the context of your age, income, job occupation, or the city you live in? These labels are important parts of who you are, but they do not represent *all* of you. If everything external and circumstantial were stripped away, who then would you be? Who are you in the privacy of your own mind, your own heart, your own dreams?

I have no doubt the answer to this question lives within you right now, even if it feels obscured or hidden. If you are struggling to locate this inner truth, I invite you to search within through more questions: What lights you up? What makes you feel alive, invigorated, and inspired? What speaks to your soul, calls to your heart, and feels like a familiar embrace to your physical body? Perhaps you were born knowing the answers to these questions, yet somewhere along the winding path of life, they slipped from your grasp and dissipated like mist on the horizon . . . either that, or you willingly released them to save yourself pain and heartache.

Much like a tender joint or a sore throat, feeling lost, stuck, or blocked is usually a symptom of some greater issue or imbalance. When we encounter a symptom we want to treat, we first have to investigate and discover the root cause. In this chapter, we will explore some of the innate beliefs and fears related to the witch wound that can cause us to feel lost, stuck, or blocked.

Limiting Beliefs

Limiting beliefs are the thoughts, ideas, and stories we tell ourselves that keep us from pursuing our dreams, fulfilling our goals, and doing the things we feel called to do. These beliefs can be about ourselves and our own abilities, but also about the world at large. For instance, you might believe you are not creative enough to be a successful writer, that you are too emotionally damaged to have a fulfilling relationship, or that you will never be wealthy because of your poor money management skills. These would all be examples of limiting beliefs about yourself.

By comparison, limiting beliefs about life or the world at large could look like the belief that people are inherently bad and cannot be trusted or the belief that modern society is corrupt and there is no point in trying to change things. In each of these examples, the underlying message is the same: because of factors outside your control, it is simply not possible for you to have the things you want to have or to do the things you want to do. This mindset is defeatist, disempowering, and a detriment to any magical or spiritual practice.

In previous chapters, we discussed some of the most common limiting beliefs that plague modern witches, pagans, and other spiritual individuals: the idea that you are too much or not enough, the belief that you will be rejected or mocked for being yourself, and the outlook that it is unsafe to speak your truth or to be authentically seen.

While there are extremely valid historical and modern cultural precedents to these limiting beliefs, it is important to evaluate them honestly and to ask the question: how true are these beliefs *really*? Let's break down the limiting idea that "It's not safe for me to talk about my belief in magic and witchcraft." How true is this belief for you *really*?

A good place to start is by defining what it means to be safe. What exactly do you mean when you say sharing your belief in magic and witchcraft is unsafe: that you might be physically harmed, that you might be kicked out of your home, that your reputation or social status might be damaged, that you might lose certain relationships, that you might be judged and mocked, or that you might have to endure uncomfortable conversations? These answers will be different for everyone, and it is important to be mindful of intersectionality. Unfortunately, coming out of the broom closet is more unsafe for some than for others. Protecting your physical and mental well-being should always come first.

Assuming you are not in a position where your physical safety or well-being is at risk, it is then important to look at the deeper implication of this limiting pattern of thought. For instance, if we dive into this idea, the underlying fear may be that your friends will judge and reject you. Going even deeper, you may discover that you doubt your ability to handle the sting of rejection or to make new friends who are more accepting. These limiting beliefs offer a more solid, concrete foundation to work from than the vague and ominous original statement of "It's not safe for me to talk about my belief in magic and witchcraft."

This is not to say you need to act in opposition to your limiting beliefs right away. Rather, as you explore your limiting beliefs and sit with the deeper fears that exist beneath the surface, you will gradually and naturally build the capacity to challenge them through your behaviors and actions.

Living for Other People

As we discussed in the previous chapter, the witch wound commonly manifests as an intense fear of authentic self-expression. It can feel much safer to transform into a toned-down version of yourself—a version that meets societal expectations and draws minimal attention from those who may feel threatened by your authenticity—than to display your true colors for all the world to see. In this way, you end up living for others rather than living for yourself.

Unfortunately, these self-protective measures can end up influencing the way we view ourselves even in the privacy of our own inner lives. Years of stifling our truths and hiding our beliefs, interests, and gifts can lead to confusion and doubt about who we really are and what we are capable of achieving. For how long can you diminish and downplay your magic in the company of others before you start to believe those lies yourself?

This is especially true when the fear of being authentically seen and heard blocks us from doing the things we truly want to do. If your dream is to become a practicing herbalist, offer tarot readings, or start a witchy podcast, but fear of being identified and recognized by the people in your "real life" prevents you from following that dream . . . well, you can see how that makes for an existence that feels restrictive and unfulfilling.

When I made the decision to open my online store and begin selling my handmade pagan ritual items, I was unbelievably excited. I felt as if all the inner work and spiritual, magical learnings I had been doing over the years had led me to that point. But I also felt terrified. How was I going to explain my new business to the friends and family who didn't yet know that I was a pagan and a witch? What if the people I had intentionally *hidden* this fact from ended up finding my online store?

Ultimately, I decided to launch my online witchy craft store despite these nagging fears and insecurities—and it has proved to be a beautiful and deeply fulfilling experience. Imagine if I had allowed my own fear to take this experience away from me? Furthermore, imagine if I had allowed my fear to stop me from speaking my truth, being seen, and publishing this book you now hold in your hands?

If you are in the habit of allowing other people's expectations and societal restrictions to dictate how you dress, the work you do, the hobbies you enjoy, the books you read, the way you decorate your home, the way you refer to yourself and your magical practices, or other aspects of your life and self-expression, your wounded inner witch may be driving this behavior. Over time this can damage your self-esteem and confidence, leading to feelings of being stuck or lost.

Fear of Imperfection

Armchair witch and *armchair occultist* are terms used to describe individuals who read extensively about spiritual and magical belief systems, yet rarely or never put their wisdom into real-life practice. While reading and acquiring knowledge are essential components of practicing witchcraft safely and effectively, the phrase "practice witchcraft" itself illuminates the heart of the matter. According to the Cambridge English Dictionary, *practice* is defined as "action rather than thought or ideas" and *craft* is defined as "something produced using skill and experience."

Indeed, the greatest mysteries of magic and witchcraft cannot be taught; they must be experienced firsthand. Why then do so many witches slip into armchair occultism? My theory is that perfectionism is to blame. We can trace this symptom back to the root fear of being too much or not enough. When we carry these limiting beliefs, we put off doing the things our hearts feel called to do.

Additionally—and largely because of Christian programming and negative stereotypes about magic and witchcraft—many witches enter the world of occultism with the belief that magic is inherently dangerous. Certainly, learning protective measures should be the first order of business for any new witch. Yet once those basics are in place, there is no reason to delay actually performing magical acts.

Generally speaking, learning to read tarot cards, practicing candle magic, and preparing healing herbal infusions are not going to invite the forces of chaos and darkness into your life. Even as you advance into more complex magic, imperfection is not inherently harmful. The moon phase and planetary hour may not always be perfectly suited to your spellwork; you may not be able to celebrate pagan festivals on their precise dates; and you may stumble through ritual scripts and mispronounce words. All of that is okay, and all of that will yield results that are infinitely more powerful than never attempting magic at all.

Perfection is not nature's way, nor is it the witch's way. Do not allow fear of imperfection to block you from following your magical path— or any other path that calls to your heart and soul. Because indeed, the witch wound is insidious; it often shows up in areas that are seemingly unrelated to magic and witchcraft.

Perhaps your ultimate dream is to write a book or launch a business, yet you continuously find what you consider valid reasons to avoid taking that first step: you do not feel knowledgeable or experienced enough to get started; you have other responsibilities that need tending; you need to get the other areas of your life in order first; and so on. These justifications are sane and rational—up to a point. Years and years of stalling your life's work is not prudent or wise, it is your witch wound holding you back.

Puritan values would have you believe that perfection is necessary to be a good and respectable person. These values teach that imperfection is rooted in sin and a sign you are not among those predestined to be saved by God. According to this system of beliefs, adhering to strict church-ordained regulations, practices, and societal norms is the only thing that can protect you from the damnation of imperfection.

Being the wise one that you are, you know in your soul that imperfection is not equivalent to damnation. Your spirit was not made to be tamed, controlled, or confined to rigid rules of conduct. Starting a new project requires moving past a known area and out onto uneven ground, and that can be a messy process. There is always more preparation that can be done, but without a clear path forward and a willingness to make mistakes along the way, preparation can become eternal procrastination.

This can feel safe for the body, but it is harmful for the soul. You exist here and now for a greater purpose than to remain stuck in the same cycles of dreaming, wishing, and waiting. If you feel called toward something more, trust that you are ready. Feel the magic and authenticity of your imperfection.

Money Fears

Fear of imperfection is not the only reason you might be stalling your dreams and ambitions. How is your relationship with money? How do you feel about the amount you earn: satisfied, happy, thrilled, anxious, depressed, ambivalent? Do you believe you are capable of earning more money than you currently do? Would you like to? How do you feel about your spending habits? How would your life change if you earned more money, earned less money, saved more money, or spent more money?

These questions can be triggering for many people, and especially for individuals carrying the witch wound. Women who earned their own income as healers and midwives faced a particularly high level of scrutiny during the Burning Times, as did women who had very little money and resorted to begging and rioting. Yet again, we see how it was unsafe for people—especially women—to be too powerful and influential, as well as not powerful and influential enough.

As the flames of patriarchy burned through Europe, midwives and herbalists were replaced by doctors, and cunning folk were replaced by priests. Even today, society shakes its head at practices such as divination, astrology, and energy healing, and many practitioners of these sacred arts grapple with shame and self-doubt about charging money for their services. When the world at large believes your gifts are fraudulent and dishonest—and when people like you were once sentenced to death for sharing those same gifts—it is naturally difficult to remain unaffected.

You might experience this manifestation of the witch wound in the form of limiting beliefs about money: that you always must choose between money and happiness, that you will never earn enough money, or that growing the amount of money you have is more difficult for you than it is for others. These limiting beliefs can shape your financial reality by influencing your money-earning and spending behaviors.

You may charge too little for your work or avoid asking for a well-deserved raise. Why? Having someone question your value can feel extremely threatening to the nervous system; playing it small feels safer and more comfortable. This can also show up as an inability to hold on to money by spending it as soon as you earn it. On some level, your psyche retains this idea that if you succeed—if you become too wealthy, too powerful, too influential—you will be targeted and harmed. So you subconsciously prevent this by ensuring you never exceed your comfortable upper limit of financial success.

This symptom of the witch wound runs deeper yet. Your soul remembers a time when those who controlled the wealth were the ones enclosing land and persecuting neighbors who spoke against this injustice, ultimately leading to their executions. This inherited memory can make the idea of accumulating money and power feel dirty and wrong, like picking up the evil tool of the witch-hunters themselves.

To this point, I ask: if you had access to more money, would you use it in a way that is harmful to yourself or others? Being the wise and empathetic soul that you are, I trust fully that you would not. I trust that you would use your money as a resource to uplift yourself and those around you. While in your power, how could money be dangerous, dirty, or wrong?

In truth, money is neither good nor evil; it is simply a tool, no different than a pen or a hammer. Like all tools, money's influence is determined by the hands that wield it. I can only imagine that Earth would be a more beautiful and peaceful place if witches, pagans, and healers collectively controlled more of the planet's money.

You were born with powerful magic within your soul, and this magic cannot be taken from you. Even as limiting beliefs and fears obscure it, your unique magic continues to radiate from within. It is yours to be tapped, utilized, and enjoyed. How are you meant to use this magic? That is not for me to tell you, but rather for you to decide—yes, *decide*.

Feeling lost, stock, or blocked is your highest self's way of signaling that a change needs to be made. Truthfully, I believe every human's soul purpose is to embody their magic and use it to shape a life that brings them happiness and fulfillment. I also believe there are infinite paths leading to this outcome. Certainly, if you are unhappy with your current means of paying the bills, it's in your best interest to explore alternate routes.

Yet your soul's purpose and your career are not inherently linked. If you feel your purpose in this lifetime is to help others and make a positive impact on the world around you, it is entirely possible to fulfill this purpose while working a nine-to-five that pays the bills. Despite what our capitalist conditioning would have us believe, the forty hours we spend earning money each week do not have to the be the hours that define us most. What we do during the other 128 hours can be just as or even more important.

In fact, your soul's purpose can be as deliciously simple as living a life devoted to your own healing and pleasure, or to cultivating a life of magic, beauty, and abundance. As you open yourself to these new ideas of what it means to fulfill your soul's purpose or live a meaningful life, you may find the sensation of being stuck or blocked gives way to a new state of flow.

The Witch Wound Can Show Up As . . .

- Feeling lost, stuck, or blocked from achieving something more in life

- Limiting your own potential in order to meet other people's expectations

- Shrinking yourself to avoid drawing attention

- Holding limiting beliefs about yourself, your abilities, or the nature of the world

- Fear of imperfection and making mistakes

- Continuously delaying your dreams and goals

- Limiting beliefs or fears about money

8

Ancestral Wounding
and Past-Life Memories

I am a witch. Today, I have the privilege of claiming that title and practicing my craft without the fear of imprisonment, torture, or death. Yet when I close my eyes and reflect on the horrors of the Burning Times, that sense of fear, pain, anger, and disgust is visceral. As I conducted research for this book, I read stories that left me shaking with rage, sobbing on the floor, or clutching my chest as adrenaline surged through my body.

These strong reactions can partially be attributed to the fact that I am an empathetic person who understands that no human should be treated the way these people were. Grief, anger, and anxiety are all natural reactions to learning about the atrocities of the past.

But it would be a mistake to dismiss the idea that the witch wound can and does impact how modern-day witches process and respond to these historical horrors. In this chapter, we will explore the threads that connect the symptoms of the witch wound to the Burning Times through the lens of inherited ancestral trauma and past-life memories.

The Ancestral Witch Wound

I do not have any knowledge of ancestral witches in my family line. More likely, most of my ancestors throughout history *feared* witches. But I do descend from individuals who lived through the Burning Times in Germany, Denmark, Sweden, England, and elsewhere in Europe. Regardless of their beliefs about magic, they lived in an era when being a witch was unsafe and punishable by death. Perhaps they witnessed trials or executions in their towns or knew someone who was accused and prosecuted.

What fears about magic and witchcraft might have haunted them in their lifetimes? What fears might have been passed down through their words and actions—as well as their DNA, their blood, and their bones—to their children, grandchildren, and great-grandchildren, eventually becoming imbedded in our lineage?

Intuitively, I do believe I have ancestors who knew fear during this time—especially on my father's side of the family. The witch wound is often assumed to be a maternal one, likely because of the perception of witchcraft as a feminine art. Yet people of all genders can be witches, and thus the witch wound can affect—and can be passed down through—people of all genders as well. While both my mother's and father's ancestors likely would have been impacted by the Burning Times in some way, I feel the wounding more strongly through my paternal line—the skepticism of magic or anything supernatural, the desire to be seen as logical and rational, and the fear of standing out, being judged, and getting into trouble.

Perhaps even more importantly, I feel quite certain that I have *recent* ancestors—grandparents, great-grandparents, and great-great-grandparents—who were mistrustful of magic and would have associated witchcraft with demonic activity. I also know these same ancestors carried emotional and spiritual wounds that were separate from the witch wound, yet manifested in ways similar to those we have previously discussed, such as fear of authentic self-expression.

Certainly, my great-grandfather who immigrated to the United States from Denmark in 1911 would have struggled with real fears about earning enough money and being successful in his new home. Likewise, my Oma (grandmother) no doubt carried a deep rejection wound and a feeling of being not enough as a result of her relationship with her in-laws. My great-grandmother was a devout Lutheran, and she never accepted my Oma as part of the family because of her Catholic beliefs. I shudder to think what my great-grandmother would have thought about *my* spiritual beliefs! Interestingly, I carried a deep fear of sharing my spiritual practices with relatives—especially my in-laws—for many years. Could the ancestral memory of my Oma's wounded relationship with her family have been the origin of this fear?

I also cannot help but wonder how long these same trauma patterns have been playing out. How many generations of my family line have been plagued by similar emotional wounds, and where did those wounds *actually* originate? Were my great-grandmother and my Oma truly the first of my ancestors to clash over religious viewpoints, or was their conflict woven from the threads of some more ancient wound—perhaps one that dates back multiple generations, even as far back as the Burning Times?

If your ancestors lived in a region of the world where witch trials were held or bias against witches existed or still exists today—which, sadly, can be said of most of the globe—you may experience this same sense of deep ancestral remembering that I have described. After all, you are the living legacy of your ancestors. Whether you know their names and stories or not, the things they did, felt, experienced, and believed in their lifetimes have shaped your present reality. Their memory lives on in the cells of your body through the DNA you inherited from them.

Epigenetic studies have demonstrated how trauma can be passed down from one generation to the next, causing children and grandchildren to relive the symptoms of traumas that they were not even around to experience.[1] This inherited trauma might be described as a kind of somatic remembering of the emotions, beliefs, and fears that our ancestors carried within their bodies, passed to us through the same DNA that gave us our father's hair color, our grandmother's nose, or our great-grandfather's sweet tooth.

While the mechanisms behind intergenerational trauma are still being studied, what we do know is that strong emotions can and do echo across generations and can impact physical, mental, emotional, and spiritual well-being. During the Burning Times of early modern Europe, an estimated fifty thousand or more individuals were executed in the most vile and unimaginable of ways, and perhaps twice as many were imprisoned, violently tortured, and exiled by their families and communities. These events unfolded across the continent over the span of multiple centuries. How many hundreds of thousands of people might have been psychologically scarred by these horrors? How many more are added to that figure when you consider the tens of thousands of witch hunts that have taken place outside of Europe?

Imagine you are a woman living in the late 1500s who has just learned that all but two women in a nearby village have been executed for witchcraft. Imagine you are the father of a young boy, watching in horror as another man and his son are burned alive for the crime of bewitching their pastor. Imagine you are an herbalist, midwife, or mage during these times and feeling the pressure of choosing between your livelihood and your life. What beliefs, fears, biases, and self-protective measures might these people have developed, then passed on to their descendants? What traumas might have been stored in the tissues of their bodies, working their way into the very DNA that now lives on through you and me?

Unfortunately, recognizing this symptom of the witch wound is not as simple as identifying a particular gene. The good news is that you do not need anyone or anything else—not even this book—to tell you whether you have inherited an ancestral witch wound. *You* are the most qualified person for this work. This is a wonderful opportunity to build from what you are learning now and practice trusting your own intuition as you reflect on the following questions:

- Did any of your ancestors live in regions where witch trials took place? How do you think these events might have affected them?

- What beliefs do you think your parents, grandparents, great-grandparents, and so on held about magic, witchcraft, spirituality, and religion?

- Do you hold any limiting beliefs, fears, or emotions that mirror those you have witnessed in your parents or grandparents?

- Do you intuitively sense that any of your ancestors might have struggled with symptoms of the witch wound, such as fears related to being seen, sharing their truths, being too much or not enough, spirituality and religion, or money?

- Do you intuitively sense that any of your ancestors might have been practitioners of magic and suffered from fear, shame, and persecution? Do you sense that any of them might have been witch-hunters or executioners?

Know that there is absolutely no requirement to have a known witch or victim of the Burning Times in your family tree to begin this work. Again, trust your gift of intuition: do you *feel* that the witch wound has been passed down to you through one or more of your ancestral lines? Do you feel that you, as well as your ancestors and your descendants, would benefit from tending this wound? Allow your body, soul, and heart to guide you to toward your truth and explore how it feels to put your faith in that answer.

Past-Life Memories

Just as there is no requirement to have an ancestor who was a known witch or victim of the Burning Times to undertake this work, there is likewise no requirement to have been a witch or victim of the witch hunts yourself in a past lifetime. However, some modern witches do indeed have memories or fragments of memories of being harmed or killed for their magical practices. Sometimes these memories are recovered during past-life regressions, and other times they appear in dreams or while meditating, journaling, or doing other healing work. Past-life memories can even be spontaneously triggered by certain events, places, or people.

Most often, these memories center around being physically harmed in some way: being tortured, strangled, hanged, burned, or drowned. They can also show up as excessive fears or intrusive thoughts about dying in one of these ways or intense visceral reactions to related situations—for instance, a surge of panic when water splashes on your face or when jewelry feels too tight around your neck. For some witches, these memories show up in the form of a somatic remembering rather than visual memories, such as tightness and burning in the throat and jaw or numbness and pain in the pelvic area without any apparent physical, medical cause.

I experienced one of these unexpected rememberings while following a guided visualization, though it took me nearly a year to forge the connection between my recovered memory and the witch wound. While moving through this visualization, a shocking scene appeared suddenly in my mind's eye: I was lying flat on my back in a golden field, looking up as large, fluffy clouds rolled across a cornflower blue sky. A man and a boy around ten years old were standing over me, wearing expressions of pure contempt. The man was holding a sharp tool that looked like some sort of shovel, which he lifted and brought down forcibly upon my throat. That is where the memory ends.

When this memory first came to me, I did not immediately connect it with the witch hunts. That said, I did recognize it as an actual event that belonged to *me*—not a vision or daydream, but a memory of something that occurred that was just as real and meaningful as any from this lifetime. Yet clearly, this memory was *not* from this lifetime. Even without the context of the witch hunts, I had a strong physical and emotional reaction to the idea that I had been harmed—seemingly beheaded— in another life. This vision felt particularly significant given the strange synchronicities that existed between the imagery of the shovel cutting my throat and my experiences in this lifetime.

Since childhood, I have been tormented by a deep fear of choking, suffocating, and being unable to breathe. One of my earliest memories is of becoming aware of the fact that I needed to breathe to stay alive. I remember the terror my five-year-old body felt when I realized that if I stopped breathing, I would die. Over the course of my life, this preoccupation with my throat and my ability to breathe developed into an obsession that has negatively impacted my life. I constantly felt the need to monitor how my throat felt (*Why is it so tight? Why does it hurt? Is it closing up? Can I breathe?*) and even began avoiding certain foods due to fear of choking.

A combination of cognitive behavioral therapy, exposure and response prevention therapy, and somatic experiencing therapy eventually helped me heal and find safety in my body and the uncertainties of life and death. If you struggle with the same or similar symptoms, I highly recommend finding a trained professional who offers one or more of these therapies. (And again, I want to stress that the work of healing the witch wound is *not* a substitute for professional therapy or medication. It wasn't until *after* I began to manage my anxiety and regulate my nervous system that I was able to truly dive into and benefit from this work.)

Yet even after learning how to manage my intrusive thoughts and lifelong anxiety, I yearned for deeper answers about *why* it had always felt so unsafe to simply exist. Why had I been haunted by the fragility of life and inevitability of death from the time I was a small child, while most other people seemingly went their entire lives without giving their own deaths much thought? What had caused this preoccupation with my throat in the first place—the obsessive thoughts about my throat closing, the constant feelings of tightness, and the compulsive need to check that I was still able to breathe?

I found some of the answers I was seeking when I recalled the image of my throat being cut by a shovel, as clear as if it were a memory from this lifetime. I found even more answers when I learned about the witch wound and listened to other witches share their own experiences with feeling unsafe in their bodies—and more specifically, having intrusive thoughts related to certain body parts: often their throats, chests, or sexual organs. When I heard a fellow witch share that she had experienced a vision of being dragged through a field by a rope tied around her neck while doing a past-life regression, the possible meaning behind my own memory clicked into place.

The more I spoke to and learned from other witches, the more I was stunned by the similarities in our stories. Like me, countless other witches and spiritual individuals had wrestled with intense, seemingly irrational fears about death and being physically harmed since childhood—despite having no personal history of that kind of violence. Like me, countless other witches experienced frequent tightness, burning, pain, or uncomfortable sensations in their throats and other body parts—despite doctors being unable to identify any physical cause. And like me, countless other witches had seen strange visions of themselves being beheaded, hanged, choked, drowned, burned, or tortured by people they did not recognize.

Some witches with wombs report feeling pain, numbness, or other uncomfortable sensations in this area. We know the Burning Times were largely used as a weapon against sexual empowerment, and that promiscuity, abortion, and having a child out of wedlock all served as the spark that ignited a witch hunt. We also know many accused witches were subjected to sexual violence. These kinds of symptoms may be a sign the witch wound exists in the womb space and that it requires energetic healing—*after* a mundane physical cause has been thoroughly ruled out, of course.

When we consider the horrific forms of violence the victims of the witch craze were subjected to—the scold's bridle, being stripped and prodded with a sharp needle in intimate areas, rape, hanging, strangling, drowning, burning—and compare them to the strange memories and physical symptoms that many modern-day witches report, it is certainly possible to weave a compelling story.

Could my lifelong preoccupation with my throat and my fear of being unable to breathe be linked to a past lifetime when I was executed for witchcraft, perhaps the one I saw in my vision? When I tune out the sound of naysayers and disbelievers, those who reject and condemn my version of spirituality and my methods of truth-seeking, I hear my highest self—and she says *yes*. This is what I feel and believe in my bones, given the information that has been made available to me thus far: that it is no coincidence that my greatest fears are so tightly interwoven with these somatic and psychic rememberings.

That said, I do hold space for other possibilities. Could this memory have instead originated from an ancestor who lived through the Burning Times? Could the memory be mine from a past lifetime, but unrelated to the witch hunts? Could the vision simply be a message from my highest self, letting me know my throat energy center needed tending? After all, tightness in the throat and difficulty speaking one's truth can both be symptoms of a blocked or dysregulated throat center.

Yes, I believe all these theories, among others, *could* explain both the vision and the physical sensations. Once again, I will ask you to set aside your desire for a concrete, irrefutable answer. The truth is, I cannot know with absolute certainty whether my experiences are related to the witch wound—but I can choose to trust in what my intuition tells me, and so can every other witch who faces these same questions.

Whether or not your ancestry can be traced to regions where witch trials occurred, and whether or not you can recall past-life memories of the Burning Times, your body, mind, and soul may bear the scars of this psychological wounding.

Over the span of generations, our spirits and nervous systems alike have been programmed to believe it is unsafe to practice witchcraft and magic. This belief lives within our own bodies, just as it lived within the bodies of our ancestors of blood and bone as well as our ancestors of spirit. But it also permeates every layer of our Western culture; it is the by-product of a society built upon patriarchal, capitalist, white supremacist values.

Beneath these deep layers of pain and trauma, I lovingly invite you to open your heart to the possibility that you were born into your lineage, your body, your lifetime for a reason. Perhaps that reason is to heal—not just yourself, but also those who came before you, those who will come after you, and the very soul of our society.

The Witch Wound Can Show Up As . . .

- Fears, limiting beliefs, or self-sabotaging behaviors cycling through multiple generations

- Memories of being a witch or of being physically harmed in a past lifetime

- Excessive fears or intrusive thoughts related to burning, drowning, or choking

- Tightness, pain, or burning in the throat and jaw unrelated to a medical cause

- Feelings of anxiety when clothing or jewelry feels tight around the neck

- Pain or numbness in the sacral space unrelated to a medical cause

9

The Wounded Feminine

In part one, we learned that 80 percent of all victims of the Burning Times were women. While this means an estimated ten thousand victims were men, make no mistake—the witch trials were in many ways a targeted attack on women, their bodies, and their feminine wisdom.

The witch-hunting handbook *Malleus Maleficarum* dedicated one-third of the text to making a case for why women are more inclined to practice malicious magic than men. Among the reasons given: that women have "slippery tongues" and lack the self-control to avoid sharing their evil knowledge with other women; that women have weak memories, and thus cannot be disciplined, and are prone to impulsiveness; that women are "feebler in mind and body" than men and are, in fact, more intellectually similar to children; and most importantly, that women's carnal lust is so insatiable that they will lay with the Devil and demons just to satisfy their own sexual desires.

The *Malleus Maleficarum* states that, in particular, women who display three specific qualities are most prone to witchcraft: lust, infidelity, and ambition.[1] In a later section, it maintains that "No one does more harm to the Catholic faith than midwives," not only because they operated in direct competition with male doctors, but also because they performed abortions—a great crime in an era where growing a strong workforce was a top priority.[2] Reading this text more than five hundred years after it was published, it is crystal clear what the *Malleus Maleficarum* truly was: carefully crafted propaganda, designed to paint a horrific picture of women who were influential, outspoken, and empowered.

Nearly every facet of femininity is attacked, ridiculed, and demonized in the pages of this handbook—aside from those that serve capitalism, patriarchy, and religion. These transgressions live on in the DNA of every woman who is alive today, passed down to them through the generations of women who came before. But they also live on in our very culture.

At this point, I feel called to acknowledge and honor certain truths about gender in the context of the witch wound: that there are witches, healers, pagans, and spiritual individuals of all genders; that gender is a spectrum and not a binary; that having certain anatomy is not what defines one's gender; and that gender is experienced differently by different people. These are sacred, timeless truths that I respect deeply.

And also, it is true that the violence of the Burning Times disproportionately affected women and that much of this violence was sexual in nature. For this important reason, our discussion of the witch wound would not be complete without examining the mark it has left upon women's psyches and bodies. While people of all genders may find value in this chapter, I do want to note that the upcoming sections will focus specifically on themes that may be most relevant for women—including, of course, transgender women—like the Sacred Feminine, female friendships, and female sexuality. Additionally, there is some discussion of anatomy such as breasts and wombs. Discussing these topics with raw honesty can be a powerful form of medicine for the countless women who carry the witch wound.

If you are not a woman but have the capacity to hold space for this feminine-centered work, we would be honored to have you join us in this chapter. If you feel that this chapter is not relevant for you or that these discussions may be triggering, please consider meeting us in the following chapter. In either case, I invite you to listen to your intuition and respect your own boundaries—two important steps in actively healing the witch wound.

Disconnection from the Divine Feminine

While conditions for women have no doubt improved dramatically in the five hundred years since the *Malleus Maleficarum* was published, it is quite shocking to reflect on what has not changed. Today, women are still criticized for expressing their sexuality on their own terms. Women are still judged more harshly than men for their sexual proclivities. Women are still vilified for procuring birth control and abortions. Women are still advised against being too ambitious or influential, and women are still mocked for their "slippery tongues" (i.e., gossiping).

An immense amount of societal and cultural pressure is placed upon women to act *more* like men, especially in professional settings. Women are routinely judged and criticized for being too emotional and for relying on personal tools such as intuition and empathy to solve problems and make decisions. Yet in the same breath, women are judged and criticized for acting *too much* like men. Consider how a female politician or employer is labeled bossy or cold when she leads with the same assertiveness and decisiveness as her male peers.

Perhaps the most pervasive of all gender double standards relates to sexuality. Women's bodies are routinely objectified and exploited in all forms of media, from magazine advertisements and TV commercials to movie posters and music videos. While female representation is generally improving in popular TV shows and movies, female characters in shows that are marketed as family-friendly are still three times more likely to be shown in revealing clothing or partially nude than their male counterparts.[3] In video games, female characters are ten times more likely to be shown in revealing clothing and nearly five times as likely to be shown with some level of nudity.[4]

This widespread acceptance of female nudity clearly does not extend off-screen, however. Few body parts are more controversial or more harshly scrutinized than the female nipple. While bare breasts are tolerated—or in certain cases, expected and celebrated—in countless movies and TV shows, women who nurse their babies in public are subjected to judgmental glares and hushed whispers. In a poll of more than four thousand Americans, only 69 percent of respondents said they believe women should have the right to breastfeed in public spaces—even though it is currently legal in all fifty U.S. states.[5]

Women and girls are routinely criticized for the clothing, makeup, jewelry, and hairstyles they choose to wear, under the assumption that their outward appearance must reflect their moral values and the number of sexual partners they have had—which, of course, is yet another metric by which women are judged far more harshly than men.

Research shows that people view highly sexually active men more positively than highly sexually active women, and that having an early sexual debut and engaging in casual sex are more likely to be rewarded in men than women.[6] This statistic is hardly surprising. Many women have their own stories of grappling with sexual shame, of wondering whether their partner count is too high, and of feeling that something must be wrong with them for fantasizing about and desiring sex. These feelings of shame, guilt, anxiety, and disgust about something so natural, sacred, and necessary are yet another sign that the collective energy of the Divine Feminine is severely out of balance.

Consider how far we have strayed from the ancient ways, when our ancestors worshipped and celebrated the bodies of women; when they viewed the womb as a sacred portal to the otherworld, through which new souls could be birthed and life could be created; when no archetype was more revered and respected than that of the Mother. Over the span of hundreds of thousands of years, these beliefs and practices were woven together into a tapestry that told the story of the Divine Feminine. This tapestry lived in the soul of every woman—the inherited sum of every female ancestor's wisdom, passed down through blood and bone.

But as the old pagan ways were wiped out, this ancient wisdom was very nearly lost. It lived on solely in the folktales and practices that were passed down in hushed whispers from grandmother to mother to daughter. By the Middle Ages, the old ways of Earth-based feminine wisdom hung only by a thread—and by the time the last suspected witch in Europe was executed, by the time the wisdom of women had been reduced to ash and smoke, that thread had been cut.

Do you feel it? Do you feel that sense of separation, of loss, of emptiness deep inside your soul, where the tapestry of Divine Feminine wisdom is meant to be? Does your heart echo with the memory of a time when female sexuality was celebrated rather than shamed, when women were the trusted wisdom keepers of all things related to pregnancy and birth, and when women gathered around the fire to unite their voices in story and song?

When women are objectified, shamed, demoralized, repressed, and abused, their innate gifts—intuition, creativity, empathy, compassion, sensuality—cannot shine forth in full power. How can women tap into the magic of their voices, their bodies, their creativity, and their psychic abilities when these are the very expressions they are being shamed for by our patriarchal society?

As with the Earth Mother herself, much of a woman's feminine power is buried deep within the caverns, hills, and valleys of her physical body. Just as disrespecting and abusing the Earth drains the Great Mother of her power, so too does relentless torment of female bodies drain each woman of her Divine Feminine magic.

Feeling Unsafe around Other Women

During the Burning Times, female friendships were a dangerous thing. Many accused witches named dozens of others as witches while they were being interrogated and tortured, often their own sisters, mothers, daughters, and female friends. Not only did the women of this era live in fear of being accused of witchcraft by the powerful men in their communities, they also feared betrayal from the women in their inner circles. Being publicly associated with other women was risky by its own right; if one of those women was identified as a witch, all eyes would turn to those closest to her. It would have been safest to avoid spending much time with other women at all.

This was a stark contrast compared to the way female friendships were viewed in the pre–witch craze medieval era, when most women lived their lives in close connection with other women. During the Middle Ages, the average woman would have spent significantly more time in the company of other women than men—even her own husband. Women tended households together, raised babies together, sewed and cooked together, and spent their leisure time together. When a woman birthed her babies into the world, it was not her husband who would have stood by her side, but rather her midwife, mother, sisters, and female companions.

But a woman who primarily leans on other women for support and empowerment is not easily controlled by the patriarchy, and thus female friendships were highly threatening to the growing patriarchal systems. Beginning in the early to mid-1500s, women were increasingly instructed to make their husbands the axis around which their worlds turned. Husbands were advised to keep their wives from visiting their families, especially their female friends, too frequently after marriage. A proclamation issued in 1547 in England forbade women from gathering to "babble and talk."[7]

Yet no act threatened the strength and sanctity of female friendships more than the witch trials. Imagine the terror a woman must have felt as she watched the women of her village be publicly beheaded, strangled, hanged, or burned alive, one after the other. Imagine the rage, despair, and sense of betrayal she must have felt when she learned that one of those women—someone she had once cared for deeply—had named her as a witch, thus sentencing her to the same gruesome fate.

Many women today struggle with forming genuine, authentic, trusting relationships with other women. Despite fighting all the same

Heal the Witch Wound

battles discussed in the previous section, women often feel threatened by the women in their social circles and are driven to compare and compete rather than collaborate. There is a certain scarcity mindset that seems to plague female relationships: the idea that there are only so many seats at the table for women—whether that table is one of career success, creative success, or relationship success—and that the only way we can claim one of those seats is by outmaneuvering the women around us. It can feel deeply intimidating and painful to see another woman succeed in achieving the things we want, especially when our own endeavors don't work out. But is that woman truly the enemy?

Many women go through a "not like other girls" phase, where they judge and criticize other women they perceive to be expressing their femininity in the wrong way. This might take the form of a working mom judging a stay-at-home mom for giving up her career, or a woman who dresses casually and does not wear makeup judging women who do dress up and wear makeup for striving to meet society's standards of attractiveness—and vice versa.

In these and other scenarios, the woman casting judgment is doing so out of the deeply ingrained belief that she is in competition with the other woman. If she expresses herself in a way that is different from another woman, then one of them must be wrong in their self-expression. Rather than focusing on the true enemy—patriarchy and misogyny—she is making an enemy out of other women. In essence, this is no different than how women were made scapegoats for all of society's ills during the Burning Times.

This mistrust of women can also show up as avoiding close relationships with other women due to the belief that they are inherently more dramatic, gossipy, unstable, or emotional than men—while also ignoring positive stereotypes about women, such as the fact that women are generally viewed as more empathetic and nurturing than men. Personally, I went through my own version of this phase as a teenager. Despite having never had a single altercation with one of my female friends, I often stated that I preferred male friendships because there was "less drama." Where did this belief come from? It was certainly not rooted in my own lived experience, yet I defended it as fiercely as if it were.

Even if you have formed close relationships with other women, the witch wound might still prevent you from fully opening up about certain experiences, beliefs, passions, or hobbies. As much as I love the women in my life, I have struggled to share the depths of my spiritual beliefs and magical practices with many of them, primarily out of fear that they will judge me and talk about me when I'm not around. But it's important to note this fear is rooted not in what has actually happened, but rather in a *possible* outcome I have created in my own mind. Would the women around me *really* whisper and laugh behind my back if I shared my magic with them? No doubt, there are some who would—but there is a strong likelihood that others, and perhaps most, would not.

Isn't it better for me to know who truly accepts me for my authentic self so I can prioritize those relationships? Imagine how fulfilling the bonds of sisterhood could be if we genuinely allowed ourselves to be seen and held by other women. Imagine how we might feel if we discovered that the women around us have all been feeling the exact same way.

There is immense beauty and sanctity in femininity. For tens of thousands of years, women served as the keepers of wisdom and memories. These strong, ancient women wove stories with their voices, connecting the past, present, and future. They sang words of praise for the female body, celebrating each woman's ability to receive the seed of vitality and birth life into the world. Their innate gifts—their intuition and their magic—were trusted and revered by the male leaders in their communities. They served as respected advisors and powerful priestesses.

Today, the energies of the Divine Masculine and the Divine Feminine are severely out of balance—and our planet is suffering for it. Masculine energy is sacred and beautiful in its own right, but when the masculine overpowers the feminine, our Earth and our way of life lose their natural equilibrium. In excess, masculine energy can be domineering, aggressive, predatory, and rapacious. The effects of this imbalance are readily apparent in our world—we see it in the decimation of nature, in racism and homophobia, in police brutality, in war, in gender inequality and sexual violence.

Our Earth and our people—of all genders—need this balance to be restored. We need the intuitive, nurturing, creative, sensual, collaborative, supportive energies of the Divine Feminine, which will in turn bring out the much-needed light attributes of the Divine Masculine: action, accountability, courage, strength, responsibility, protection. Imagine the kind of world we could create if all these energies were directed at healing the Earth, healing our modern culture, and healing our people's bodies, minds, and spirits.

I believe this form of healing begins with embracing the three great archetypes of the Sacred Feminine, often depicted in the form of a Triple Goddess: the Maiden, Mother, and Crone. If we can befriend and honor these manifestations of femininity within not just ourselves, but also those around us and the universe as a whole, we can begin the important work of healing the wounded feminine and reawakening the ancient bonds of sisterhood.

In a paradoxical twist, I find hope and inspiration in these words from the *Malleus Maleficarum*: "If we inquire, we learn that nearly all the kingdoms of the world have been overthrown by women."[8] I, for one, look forward to seeing the world that awaits us when our current system has been effectively overthrown.

The Witch Wound Can Show Up As . . .

- Feeling separated or disconnected from the Divine Feminine
- Grief for the loss of ancient Divine Feminine knowledge and practices
- Rejecting femininity in yourself, in others, or in our collective culture

- Feelings of shame about your body, especially your breasts, vulva, vagina, or womb

- Feelings of shame about your sexuality or sexual desires

- Feeling unsafe or uncomfortable around other women

- Feelings of competition or jealousy in response to other women

Part Three

HEALING THE
WITCH WOUND

Magical soul, we have traveled far in our journey together. We have walked through the shadows of the past, opening our hearts to the grief and rage of the Burning Times. We have likewise navigated the darkness of our own inner shadows, exploring our individual wounds, fears, and limiting beliefs together. By this point, it is my sincere hope that you understand why the witch wound exists and how it manifests in your own life.

These learnings are the ingredients we will add to the cauldron of the witch wound. For now, they are just that: ingredients. But over the course of the following chapters, you will learn how to stir these ingredients together within our great cauldron to concoct a powerful healing potion—one that is uniquely suited to you. The third and final section of this book will guide you through both practical exercises and deeply magical, spiritual rituals that will help you heal the witch wound as it manifests within your own body and spirit.

Through these pages you will tend to your spiritual scars by clearing away old, stagnant energies and patterns that no longer serve you and by calling in self-empowerment and support. You will learn to deepen your connection with your ancestors, the living Earth, your inner feminine, and your own physical body. These practices will guide you toward the greater objective of reclaiming your power, honoring your magic, celebrating your uniqueness, and embodying your authentic soul expression.

With this book as the altar, I have offered you many of my most cherished rituals and practices to aid in the work of healing the witch wound. It is up to you, magical soul, to take the offerings that resonate and leave the rest—but it is also up to you to follow through and act. You may choose to work through each of these rituals and exercises as you read, or you may prefer to come back to some of them at a later time. Either route is perfectly fine, as long as you are *actually* doing the work. Additionally, these rituals can always be repeated in the future as you progress along your healing journey.

Before we begin, I feel called to remind you that the path of healing is rarely smooth. It can be beautiful and joyful at times, but may just as likely be challenging, uncomfortable, scary, and painful. Do not fear these moments of darkness, for they create the greatest opportunities for growth. Each time you are met with resistance and find a way to persevere, each time you feel those familiar senses of shame and fear and choose to respond in a different way—*that* is when the magic of healing happens. This process is how you break your current cycle of trauma and repattern your nervous system to create real, lifelong changes.

One final time, let us breathe together. As you inhale deeply, imagine that you are breathing in pure, sacred healing light. As you hold your breath, see this light swirling throughout the cavity of your body, touching every cell. Finally, as you exhale, allow this light to return to the universe, carrying with it any and all energies that will not serve you on the path ahead. Trust that these energies will be renewed by the universe, by Source, by the Divine, or by whatever power you believe in.

Now, magical soul, it is time to embark on the last stage of our journey. It is time to stir the cauldron of the witch wound. It is time to heal.

10

Clearing Energetic Space

When you want to improve the energy or atmosphere of your home, what is the first thing you do? For many of us, the answer is cleansing—whether on a mundane level, a magical level, or both. It doesn't matter if you are decluttering the counters and sweeping the floors or lighting incense, cleansing generates the same effect: it clears out the old and makes space for the new.

Just as your home can collect unwanted energies—from guests, previous tenants, and even the energy brought in from the outside world after a stressful day—your own energetic field can also hold on to negative energies that are not serving your highest purpose. These energies can be picked up from the people you interact with, the media you consume, and the places you spend your time, but they can also be generated by your own fears, worries, and limiting beliefs.

Likewise, just as cleansing and creating space is the first step toward inviting more positive, healing energy into your home, it is also the first step in releasing the witch wound's hold over your life. Feeling afraid or ashamed of your true nature can energetically block you from abundance, confidence, pleasure, and inner peace. By tending to the fears and limiting beliefs that are keeping you afraid, lost, stuck, and blocked, you can create the space needed to draw more magic and healing energy into your life.

This is not an instantaneous process, nor is it one that should be rushed. There is no single ritual that will enable you to transition from a mindset of scarcity and fear to one of liberation and abundance overnight. However, as with any journey, awareness is the first step. By becoming aware of your own energetic blockages, you can begin to gently push and pull, loosening them little by little to clear more space gradually. You might be surprised how powerful the results of creating even just a bit more energetic space in your life can be. And remember—if a certain belief, action, or pattern is costing you your peace, then it costs too much. The time to let it go is *now*.

Ideas for Releasing and Cleansing

Just as there are many ways to cleanse the energy of your physical space, there are infinite methods you can use to loosen the bonds of the witch wound and clear away that which holds you back. Below are several of the methods that have been most helpful in my own journey of healing the witch wound.

Take a Cleansing Ritual Bath or Shower

Have you ever noticed how refreshed and rejuvenated you feel after washing yourself? Water not only clears away the physical dirt, sweat, and grime from your body, it also purifies and cleanses your energetic field. Preparing a ritual bath or shower is a simple yet effective way to loosen and wash away stagnant energy that is no longer serving you. You can amplify these cleansing benefits by adding Epsom salts to your bathwater or by using a gentle salt scrub on your body, as salt is associated with purification and protection.

After entering the tub or shower, call upon the elements of water and earth (if using salt) to aid you in this ritual. As you shower or soak, reflect on the key symptoms of the witch wound that keep you tethered to the trauma of the Burning Times and unable to move forward. Visualize this trauma as a web of black energy within and around your body. Then see this web of negativity being loosened by the salt and washed away by the water. Once all the negative energy has been cleared away, see and feel your body glowing with a soft white light. Allow the water to drain completely from the tub. Repeat anytime you feel yourself carrying energies and emotions that are not serving you.

Return Unwanted Energy to the Earth

If you are someone who often absorbs the energy of the people and environments around you—as many empaths and highly sensitive people do—it is important to regularly clear your energy field and release that which does not belong to you. Why? When we hold on to energy we have picked up from other people and places, we can become confused about our own emotions, wants, and needs, thereby delaying our healing process.

One way to do this is through a form of grounding or earthing. You will need to be outside to do this, and preferably barefoot. Plant your feet firmly on the ground and stand up tall, with your spine straight and lengthened from your tailbone to the top of your head. Alternatively, you may sit in a chair with your feet upon the ground. Take a few slow, deep breaths in and out to calm your nervous system and to ease into a relaxed state.

Imagine or sense the soles of your feet buzzing and tingling with life energy. Then feel that energy stretching out from your feet like roots, down into the Earth. Picture your energetic roots breaking through the ground or floor, the soil, the bedrock, and each subsequent layer of the Earth, growing deep and wide. Now reflect on the emotions or energy that you want to clear away, and begin sending that energy down your trunk, down your legs, and out through the soles of your feet.

Allow this unwanted energy to flow out through your roots deep into the Earth, far away from your physical body. Here the immense pressure and heat of the planet will transmute this negative energy back into raw life energy that can be recycled and used in new ways. When you are done sending away unwanted energy, feel pure Earth energy running up your roots into your feet, filling your entire body with a sense of calm and quiet strength. Allow yourself to attune to the Earth and its attributes: stability, perseverance, groundedness. When you are ready to end this visualization, imagine your roots disconnecting from the Earth and receding back up into the soles of your feet.

Perform a Cord-Cutting

Often our own fears, self-judgments, and limiting beliefs stem from the words and actions of the people around us. For instance, if you grew up in a strict religious household where magic and witchcraft were condemned, those fears and judgments may live on not only in your memories, but also embedded in your energetic field.

A cord-cutting ritual can be used to sever ties between yourself and another person, but also between yourself and a certain place, object, or even fears and beliefs. There are several ways to perform a cord-cutting ritual. The first method involves envisioning an energetic cord connecting you and the person or thing you wish to sever ties with. In your mind's eye, see a sharp knife or a pair of scissors cutting this cord and each person's energy being returned to them.

Alternatively, you can use sympathetic magic—a type of magic that involves using physical items to represent a person or thing—to sever this energetic cord. To do this, you will need yarn or string, scissors, and two objects—one representing yourself and the second representing the person or thing you wish to cut ties with. Consider using photos, candles, or other disposable objects for this ritual. Tie one end of the string around the first object and the other end around the second, leaving a few inches of string between the two items. As you do this, focus your mind on the real-life energetic connection that already exists between yourself and whomever or whatever you are cutting ties with.

Finally, use your scissors to the cut the string or yarn and, when you do, feel the severing of that energetic exchange reflected in the real world.

Heal the Witch Wound

Dispose of all materials outside your home, such as in a public dumpster or a trash can on the street.

Strengthen Your Boundaries

Boundary-setting is an important part of creating energetic space. Knowing how to shed and release external energy that has attached itself to you is important, but equally essential is knowing how to stop that energy from permeating your energetic field in the first place.

Personal Boundaries

Often when we hear the word *boundaries*, we think of something restrictive, limiting, and negative. I challenge you to reframe the way you think about boundaries by considering this point: boundaries of all kinds are useful—even necessary—for creating not just separation, but also safety and security. Just as a railing can protect someone from falling off a steep cliff or the walls of your home shield you from weather and intruders, your own personal boundaries can protect your physical, emotional, mental, and energetic well-being.

When we set and maintain boundaries with the people around us, we let them know how they can best love and support us. *Whew!* That is a wildly powerful and sacred gift. It's also true in reverse—when someone sets a boundary with us, they aren't rejecting us; rather they are letting us know that they trust and value us enough to share their authentic needs. If they didn't, they wouldn't bother setting that boundary at all—they would simply shut down or leave.

Unfortunately, most of us were not raised to view boundaries this way. As children, we are taught to hug and kiss our relatives even when we don't want to (a physical boundary violation), to apologize even when we don't mean it (an emotional boundary violation), and to worship the gods our parents tell us to worship even when we don't believe in them (a spiritual boundary violation). Certainly, parents don't teach their children these things because they mean any harm. Still, the message to children is clear: your needs and wants are less important than meeting societal expectations and making the people around you feel comfortable.

As adults, we are taught to discount our own boundary needs even further. How many times in your life have you felt obligated to say yes to a friend's invitation to spend time together when you'd rather stay home, to sit politely through a triggering conversation, or even to be physically intimate with someone when you didn't entirely want to? We do these things because we want to keep the peace or because we feel pressured to meet someone else's expectations—even at the expense of our own well-being. Over time this can lead to feeling burned out, frustrated, and resentful. This is why learning how to set and maintain boundaries is so important. The key is to start becoming aware of your own needs, then to begin enforcing them in situations and with people that feel safe.

A good way to begin nurturing your boundaries is by reflecting on both the things you need from other people and the things you will not tolerate from other people. These are often two sides of the same coin. For instance, you may need to feel that your partner speaks to you respectfully at all times, including when they are angry. This can mean not tolerating being yelled at or spoken to in a sarcastic tone. Other examples of personal boundary-setting include not allowing family members to make comments about your weight, physically stepping back when someone is standing too close to you, asking your partner to help with more household chores, or avoiding social media for two hours before bed.

Boundary-setting can be deeply healing for your wounded inner witch, especially in the throat energy center. Every time you set and defend your boundaries, you also speak your truth and allow your authentic self to be seen. As you practice this and learn that it is safe to express yourself and to set boundaries, your brain will generate and strengthen new neural pathways that support this behavior. This process enables you to rewire your brain, heal your nervous system, and clear out old blockages.

Examples of Setting Boundaries

- "I love you and I'm here for you, but I'm feeling burned out and right now isn't a good time for me to have this conversation. Can I call you tomorrow?"

- "I know you feel hurt, but I am not okay with being yelled at. I'm going to take a break from this conversation right now, and we can try again in half an hour."

- "Thanks for the invitation! I would love to meet up, but tonight doesn't work for me. How about Thursday?"

- "This room is my private space. If you need something, please knock on the door and wait for me to respond before coming in."

- "Thank you for offering to help, but I actually prefer to cook on my own. I'll let you know when everything is ready."

Energetic Boundaries

Another way to think about boundaries is in terms of energetic boundaries. Just as the skin serves as a physical boundary for the body, each person's psyche is protected by a barrier that shields against harmful or unwanted external energies. Have you ever noticed that when someone else is having a bad day, you can *feel* that energy radiating from them? When our energetic boundaries are weak, other people's moods, emotions, and energetic states can impact our own in extreme ways. You may feel like you absorb or take on the energy of people around you, experience confusion about whether an emotion belongs to you or to someone else, or generally feel overwhelmed or bombarded by other people's energies and emotions. These are all signs that your energetic boundaries need reinforcement.

One simple yet powerful way to reinforce your energetic boundaries is by casting a sphere of protection around yourself using an affirmation—remember, words cast spells!—and visualization. Speak the following words out loud:

"I am [state your name], and I am shielded from all energy that does not belong to me."

As you speak these words, visualize a sphere of white light glowing inside your body cavity a few inches above your navel, in the solar plexus energy center. See this sphere growing outward in every direction until it surrounds you completely. This is your energetic boundary, and any unwanted external energies will be blocked from passing through it. Spend a few moments holding and strengthening this image in your mind's eye and feeling yourself surrounded by your own protective energy. This safe space of your own making is one that you can return to again and again, whenever you feel overwhelmed by the external world. The more you practice creating and reinforcing your sphere of protection, the stronger and more long-lasting it will become. If you struggle with forming this visual in your mind's eye or are not visually oriented, you can describe the process out loud and declare that your energetic boundary has been fortified. You can also do this exercise with more sensation-based prompts—for instance, by feeling the warmth of the protective sphere, physically sensing it expanding, or hearing it hum as it surrounds you.

Placing certain crystals around your home and wearing jewelry made from protective stones can also strengthen your energetic boundaries. Black tourmaline, onyx, obsidian, tigereye, amethyst, and fluorite are all good crystals for energetic shielding and protection.

Journal Prompts for Letting Go and Creating Space

Journaling can be a deeply powerful tool in the work of healing the witch wound, particularly in the context of releasing old patterns that hold you back and cause you to dim your own light, silence your own voice, and stifle your own magic.

As you work through these journal prompts, try to record whatever comes to mind without editing yourself. Trust that the thoughts coming through are messages from your highest self, pointing you in the direction of what most needs to be healed. Don't worry about coming up with a perfect answer; you can always come back to the same prompts multiple times.

1. Where are you holding guilt or shame? This could be about something you have done or something you have not done. What do you believe needs to happen for you to release this guilt or shame? Are there steps you can take to make this happen?

2. When you were a child, what did you want to be when you grew up? Why? What caused your mind or life path to change as you grew up?

3. What do you believe you are incapable or unworthy of achieving? Write it down. (Example: "I believe I am incapable of starting a successful business.") Now, imagine the exact opposite of that belief is true, and write it down. (Example: "I believe I am capable of starting a successful business.") You don't have to fully believe this opposite statement is true in this moment—just be open to it and imagine how you would feel if it were true. Then reflect on what is currently preventing this from being true. (Example: "I don't have enough knowledge or experience.") Are there any possible work-arounds or steps you could take to overcome this obstacle? (Example: "I could read a book or attend a workshop about starting a business.")

4. Imagine that tomorrow morning, you wake up and realize everything has changed for the better. What has changed? Describe this change, as well as what your life would look like, in as much detail as possible.

5. What is the biggest thing that is draining your energy right now? Is it possible to create more space or set more boundaries between yourself and this thing? (Examples: If work is draining your energy, could you set boundaries around when you check emails? If a relationship at home is draining your energy, could you carve out more alone time?)

6. In what kinds of situations are you most likely to repress your truth—to say yes when you mean no or to resort to people-pleasing behaviors? Think about where you are and what people you are with. What are you feeling in these moments—fear, panic, discomfort, awkwardness? How does it feel when you stifle your truth? By comparison, how do you imagine you would feel if you dared to speak your truth?

7. How would you describe your relationship with your body? Do you have a better relationship with certain body parts than others? Which body parts give you the most trouble? Can you find any feelings of gratitude for those parts of you?

8. Which people do you believe you cannot be your true, authentic self around? What would happen if you allowed this person or these people to witness the real you? How would they respond? What would that mean for your relationships? How would this impact your day-to-day life?

9. To what extent is your self-worth tied to what other people think about you? To what extent is it tied to what you think about yourself?

10. If you knew you would be accepted and celebrated for exactly who you are by the people who matter most to you, how would your life change? What about if you could be accepted and celebrated for exactly who you are by *yourself*?

FULL MOON RITUAL FOR CLEARING
AND RELEASING

The full moon is a powerful time for performing magic, especially rituals and spells related to releasing and letting go. Not only does the full moon's energy amplify magical workings, but symbolically this is an auspicious time for cleansing and clearing unwanted energy from your own life. Each day after the full moon, the moon wanes little by little until it eventually diminishes entirely and reaches the new moon phase. By aligning our own magic and intentions with the phases of the moon, we can pull from this ancient source of celestial power to create change in our lives.

Timing: Perform this ritual on the full moon, ideally at night after the sun has set and the moon has risen.

Location: I recommend performing this ritual outdoors with a view of the full moon. However, this ritual can also be performed indoors or on a cloudy evening—simply open the curtains to ensure you have a view of the night sky, even if the moon itself is obscured.

Tools: You will need a black chime candle, a candleholder, and a lighter or matches.

Before beginning the ritual, make any additional preparations you prefer—such as dimming the lights, playing meditative music, or lighting candles.

Then, energetically cleanse and bless your ritual space using your preferred method—such as burning incense, ringing a bell, or drawing out negative energy with a crystal. If you do not have any energy-cleansing tools available, you may visualize and sense a white ball of light glowing inside your solar plexus and expanding outward into a protective white sphere. Whichever method you use, state your intention to cleanse and protect your ritual space, thereby making it sacred and separating it from the mundane world.

When you are ready, open the ritual by taking a comfortable seat of your choice. Close your eyes and take three deep, slow inhales and exhales, inviting your physical body to relax and any mental chatter to fade away.

With your eyes still closed, imagine that you are standing at the top of a spiral staircase. In your mind's eye, you begin following the staircase down, down, down. See your feet landing on each step and your hand tracing the railing. Eventually, you reach the bottom of the staircase and arrive at your personal place of power; this might be a peaceful forest clearing beneath a star-filled sky, a crystalline cave in shades of amethyst and sapphire, or a cozy room with a crackling fire and plush seating. Spend a few moments taking in as much detail as you can, feeling yourself settled in this safe and sacred place.

When you feel ready, call forth your wounded inner witch—the part of your psyche that deeply longs for magical empowerment and spiritual ful-fillment, but is bound and scarred by the trauma of the witch wound. Invite them to join you in this place of power. Let the image of this part of yourself unfold in your mind's eye. Then ask your wounded inner witch what they would like to share with you, and listen to what they have to say. What are they most afraid of? What is holding them back—self-doubt, people-pleas-ing habits, scarcity mindset, pressure to conform, fear of failure? What do they need to let go of to progress along their soul journey?

As your wounded inner witch speaks their truth, let these fears and lim-iting beliefs reverberate through you. Notice and name the emotions that arise, such as grief, loneliness, rage, bitterness, frustration, or anxiety. Honor the reality of these emotions by allowing yourself to feel them deeply and fully. This is not a time to hold back; as your wounded inner witch speaks to you, let your heart crack open and spill your pain into the night so that the healing light of the full moon may cleanse and nurture these tender parts of your soul.

When they have shared all they needed to share, thank your wounded inner witch for trusting you with their truth. Leave this place of power the way you entered by returning up the spiral staircase, allowing your con-sciousness to gradually return to your physical body.

Now, open your eyes. Pick up the black candle and wrap both hands around it, grasping it tightly. As you hold the candle, imagine all the fears and painful emotions that your wounded inner witch named swirling around inside the cavity of your body like dense black smoke. See any energetic blockages or stuck energy in the crevices of your body being loosened and sucked into this swirling mass of negative energy.

Send that energy down your arms and out through the palms of your hands, into the black candle. Feel your wounded inner witch's deepest fears and heaviest emotions draining out of you and being absorbed completely by the candle. Swaying or rocking may help with this; you may also naturally feel the need to shake, cry, or scream. Trust your body to guide you, and resist the urge to force anything or hold back. Feeling deeply and honestly is an important step in processing and releasing this stuck energy.

When you sense that everything you wish to release has been expunged into the candle, place it securely in the candleholder. Light the candle and speak the following words:

"I release and banish all energy that binds me, blocks me, and prevents me from claiming my full power."

As the candle burns, the flame will purify and release all the negative energy the candle has absorbed, returning it to the universe to be recycled and renewed. Allow the candle to burn down completely in a safe place, out of the reach of pets and children and away from curtains, rugs, or other flammable materials.

If you feel spacey or woozy after this releasing ritual, ground your energy by standing or sitting with your feet on the ground and imagining roots growing out from the soles of your feet, burrowing through the floor and into the Earth beneath you. Sense these roots growing deep and spreading out into the soil. On each exhale, send excess energy out through the roots and into the Earth; as you inhale, draw stabilizing Earth energy up through the roots. Spend several moments breathing this way.

The process of working though deeply held limiting beliefs and clearing energetic blockages is not something that happens in a single ritual or journaling session. The deeper you delve into this work, the more layers of wounding you may discover. Tend to each of these as you move forward, repeating the full moon ritual and other exercises above as often as needed. While it is not an instantaneous process, you may still begin to feel the effects of this work right away, sensing that you are lighter, less constricted, and more open. As you create more energetic space, you simultaneously make room for more magic in your life.

Conjuring Self-Empowerment

As you continue working through blockages and clearing away the old, stagnant energies that are holding you back, you can begin to fill that newly created space with thoughts, beliefs, and energies that support your magic and help you feel empowered and connected. No matter what label you use to describe your spiritual beliefs and magical practices, trust that you are powerful enough to call in energies and allies that will guide you in your journey to heal the witch wound and step more fully into your magic.

Tend Your Inner Flame

When was the last time you truly tended your inner flame—that fire in your belly that burns with creative, passionate, sensual, courageous, actionable energy? When was the last time you turned your gaze inward and sat before this flame, nurturing it and reveling in its light, its warmth, its wild beauty?

We all have an inner fire that burns within us, but like all flames, it requires tending. When you neglect your inner fire and let it burn low, you might experience a lack of energy, inspiration, motivation, creativity, passion, confidence, and empowerment. Over time, this can leave you feeling lost, stuck, and blocked from your most authentic soul expression.

Fortunately, reigniting your inner spark is no more complicated than lighting a candle; all you need to do is strike the match. Right now, place one or both hands over your lower belly, just below your navel. Breathe deep into this part of your belly, and as you do, imagine a small flame burning brightly within. See this flame growing larger and larger so that light and warmth radiate from your sacral energy center. Ask your highest self and your spiritual guides to help you tend this divine flame through your daily actions, spoken words, and thoughts.

One of my favorite ways to tend my inner flame is through embodied movement. During those times when I feel my fire burning low, I have a practice of dimming the lights, turning on soulful, sensual music, and letting my body show me how it wants to move. Despite having no training as a dancer, I am always amazed by how my body is able to communicate through dance. Sometimes my back wants to arch and my hips want to open wide, and other times my arms want to stretch for the sky and my neck wants to grow long. With no mirrors, no audience, and no expectations, I am free to let my mind intelligence yield to my body intelligence—and there is so much healing power in this state of being.

Not only is embodied movement deeply healing and beneficial for the physical body, but it also stimulates the flow of energy—including the fiery energies of creativity, passion, courage, inspiration, and sensuality. Ask your body to show you what it wants to share, then simply let it move in whatever way feels good. It's okay if you don't experience any major insights or shifts right away—but don't be surprised if you do. I like to keep a journal handy to jot down emotions and thoughts that bubble up from deep within during my embodied dance practice.

Mine for Creative Gems

Often when we feel blocked from our magic or lost on our path forward, it isn't a matter of not having great ideas or aspirations. Rather, it's an issue of routinely ignoring those glimmers of inspiration instead of taking the time to notice and nurture them. Science tells us the average person has upward of 6,000 thoughts per day. While most of these thoughts are centered around mundane tasks and responsibilities like how to respond to an email or what to eat for breakfast, some are much more meaningful and powerful. It's a bit like mining for precious gems—while most of the thoughts you sift through each day aren't worth much, when something shiny or beautiful catches your eye, you need to act quickly and grab it.

I spent much of my own life feeling lost, stuck, and blocked in various ways, especially those related to my career. Despite being an imaginative, empathetic, passionate, and hardworking person—not to mention, someone with a tenth house Capricorn stellium—I spent my twenties struggling to find my career footing. Years after earning my bachelor's degree, I still had no idea what I actually wanted to do with my life—or at least, I couldn't figure out how to make what I *truly* wanted to do my reality.

The truth is, I had known for quite a long time that my ultimate dream was to leverage my creativity, curiosity, and empathy to design a career path that was entirely my own—one that would enable me to work for myself while helping others *and* positioning my fascination with the mysteries of life at the forefront. That vision of making a living through my art and my magic has always lived within me. Yet I believed this dream was far too impractical, so like many others with big dreams, I didn't pursue it.

Unsurprisingly, I also never felt truly fulfilled by the work I did. Although I had built a moderately successful freelance copywriting business, quite frankly, I often felt like a failure. I knew I wasn't doing what I *really* wanted to be doing, and that I had deeper gifts to offer the world.

But I also felt lost and unsure about how to get where I wanted to go. In spite of my strong imagination, my mind seemed to be entirely devoid of viable solutions.

My mind *seemed* to be blank, but it wasn't. The problem wasn't that the creative ideas weren't there, but that I simply wasn't listening to them. When I became conscious of this underlying issue and shifted my behaviors, things began changing rapidly. The turning point came one morning several years ago when I was lying in bed, resting in that liminal state between awake and asleep. An intriguing thought came to me, and rather than letting it drift away and sinking back into sleep—as I have done countless times throughout my life—I rolled over, picked up my phone, and made a note to myself.

This simple action proved to be tremendously impactful. By capturing my thought rather than letting it flow in and out of my brain, I created an opportunity to come back to it later to reflect, edit, and build it out. Soon I began writing *everything* down—every half-baked idea, every spark of inspiration, every small question that piqued my curiosity.

In a matter of weeks, I was stunned by how many ideas I had curated. Many of them came to me as I was lying in bed on the verge of falling asleep. Others came while I was cooking dinner, folding laundry, or watching TV with my husband. No matter what I was doing when the ideas came, I immediately stopped to jot them down. Sometimes the thoughts flowed too quickly for my fingers to keep up, so I recorded voice memos instead.

Before long, I had a list of ideas that sent a surge of joy and hope through my body every time I looked at it. One of these ideas was to channel my love of paganism and witchcraft into a business and begin selling my handmade ritual tools and workbooks online—a passion project that now generates more revenue than some of my freelance copywriting contracts. Another was to launch a workshop or write a book about a core wound that has haunted me throughout my lifetime. I am humbled and honored to say that you now hold the manifestation of that idea in your hands.

Other ideas have been simpler and less impactful, such as new witchy items to add to my shop or topics to write about on my blog Mage By Moonlight. Yet even these small creative sparks have brought so much magic into my life. I also want to emphasize that many of these ideas have nothing to do with my career or income at all; some are simply new hobbies to explore, rituals and workings to complete, and ways to call magic, joy, and adventure into my life. And of course, many of these ideas are still growing within my creative womb, waiting to be birthed into existence when their time comes.

Imagine if I had let those rare gems of ideas slip away rather than capturing them and tending them. Imagine the number of equally promising ideas that have slipped through my brain—and through yours—over the entirety of our lifetimes.

Right now, before you read any further, pick up your phone and open the notes app. Start a new note and title it "What Lights Me Up." Use this space to write down everything that sparks something within you—things you love, things that motivate you, creative ideas, rituals or spells you want to do, inspirational words, possible solutions to problems you are facing, and more. What makes this different from a journal is that you are preserving key insights from moments of clarity in the exact moment you are experiencing them.

While much of what you write down may later prove to be unimportant, some of it will be gold—and these precious nuggets will help you get unblocked and start on a more fulfilling, empowering, embodied, and aligned path.

Attune to Your Abundance

A number of years ago, I visited an energy healer with the intention of gaining more clarity about my direction in life. I had been feeling lost and stuck, unable to move forward, and was hoping to clear away whatever was blocking my intuition and divine guidance from coming through. After the session, this healer sat me down and told me that my problem was *not* that I didn't know what direction to take, but rather that I wasn't allowing myself to feel the truth of what I already knew. She told me that my intuition was sharp, and that divine guidance was in fact coming through—I simply wasn't allowing myself to listen and receive it.

With time, I came to realize that this healer was exactly right. My issue was never one of not knowing what I wanted; rather, it was a matter of fear—fear of failure, fear of looking foolish, fear of not being good enough. As I worked to shed layer after layer of this fear, I realized an important truth: I never needed to worry about not being good enough, because I am right for the things that are right for me. The things that call to my heart—magic, healing, creativity, writing, ancestral wisdom, folklore, spirituality—do so for a reason: because I am a vessel through which those things desire to be expressed. The only thing blocking me was my own fear. To get unstuck, I had to stop attuning to my fear and begin attuning to the energies of abundance, prosperity, and enoughness—all things that already existed in my life but were being overshadowed by fear and doubt.

The same is absolutely true for you, magical soul. *You* are right for the things that feel right to you. What calls to your heart? What does your heart joyfully say yes to? Open your mind to the wisdom of your heart as it shows you the answers to these questions. These may be the same interests and passions that have brought you joy since childhood. Spend some time reflecting and journaling about what comes up for you.

As you do so, you may experience inner resistance—feelings of not being enough or thoughts about why your dreams and desires are not realistic. To help you work through this resistance, start a new page in your journal and write a list of all the small daily rituals you already do or can begin doing to help you attune to the energies of abundance, prosperity, and enoughness.

Think about things that make you feel good, that make you feel powerful, that make you feel grateful. This list might include using your tarot cards, going for an evening walk, cuddling with your pet, drinking tea, practicing magic, listening to your favorite podcast, crafting, lifting weights, gardening, or eating a piece of chocolate. Feel how much magic, joy, and creativity already exists in your life! What you focus on and put your energy into becomes your reality; by attuning to all of the abundance you already have, you will begin to subconsciously realize that abundance is more attainable than you may have initially believed. This is an important step in overcoming a scarcity mindset and attracting *more* of what you love into your life.

Embrace the Spirit of Play

I can unequivocally say that I do strange and unusual things sometimes. Giving my plants names and speaking to them like friends, casting spells, stripping naked and dancing in the moonlight, praying to gods that most people believe only exist in ancient myths, donning ritual garb and calling upon the elements—yes, as meaningful as each of these acts is to me personally, there is no denying that they are strange and unusual by society's standards.

And yet . . . so what? Does it matter? Poll a randomly selected person on the street, and there is a strong likelihood they will agree with the notion that modern society has some major issues that need to be sorted out. So why are we all trying so hard to fit into that broken society? I remember sitting in my bedroom one day during the early years of my practice, feeling extremely silly about the fact that I needed to chant certain words out loud during the ritual I was doing. *What if someone hears me through the walls?* Despite my understanding of what a powerful practice chanting can be, in that moment I still felt like a child playing a game of pretend. Then it dawned on me: *who cares?*

Even if that were all there is to our magical and spiritual practices (it's not, but *if* it were), playing pretend has proven mental, emotional, and even physical health benefits for adults as well as children. Imagining that we are somewhere calm and tranquil can ward off an anxiety attack and even trigger positive physical changes like lowering our heart rate and blood pressure. Fantasizing about made-up worlds can nurture our creativity. The point is, there is absolutely nothing wrong with embracing the spirit of play and doing things for the simple sake of fun as an adult—in fact, I believe the world would be a much healthier place if we all did exactly that.

I say all of this not because I believe my spiritual or magical practices are a form of pretending—quite the opposite in fact: like millions of others, I know them to be incredibly powerful and real—but because I want to reinforce the idea that it's *okay* to be strange—or at least to be perceived that way by other people. I not only give you permission to embrace your unusual interests without shame or guilt; I encourage you to. Let your weirdness be a source of magic!

When you own who you are and stand tall in your authenticity, people recognize that. It doesn't guarantee they will see eye to eye with you, but it does show them they have no power to tear you down or make you feel ashamed. Not to mention, when you are truly tapped into the Divine and living your authentic soul expression, *that* becomes the most important thing. Who cares what your nosy neighbor or judgmental relative thinks when you are following your truth and doing work that feels deeply healing, powerful, and meaningful?

Likewise, I encourage you to bring the spirit of fun and play into your magic. While there are certainly serious aspects to both spirituality and witchcraft, they can also be exploratory and lighthearted. When was the last time you used your magic in a way that felt joyful, exciting, thrilling, pleasurable, or even sensual? Just as rituals can be used to connect with spirit guides, acquire esoteric wisdom, or heal energetic wounds, they can also be used to fill your life with more of what you love.

Enchant your herbs and spices to make your food taste even more delicious! Charge your sex toys in the moonlight to enhance your erotic pleasure in the bedroom! Create a talisman for calling adventures and unique experiences into your life! Perform a candle spell to help you embrace the spirit of rest and relaxation! All of these ideas position pleasure over productivity and can help you undo and heal from your capitalist, patriarchal conditioning.

Another way to embrace the spirit of play is through the art of pretending. Think of an archetype or character who embodies the traits that you find powerful and meaningful. You might choose a forest witch who lives in a charming cottage and prepares healing elixirs with foraged herbs, a powerful mage who wields their influence and authority to shape the world to their will, or an insightful diviner who is always reading the stars and orating prophecies. Spend an hour, an afternoon, or even an entire day role-playing as this character or archetype. What would they wear? How would they speak? The only goal of this practice is to step outside of yourself and into a role that feels exciting and empowering. Play, explore, and just see what happens.

Become the Hero of Your Story

Think about the hero from a book, movie, or TV show you love. Does this character live a charmed life where nothing bad ever happens to them and they never struggle to make the right decision? This is rarely the case. More likely, the reason this character is seen as the hero is *because* of the challenges they face. Self-doubt, fear, obstacles, and failures are all part of the hero's journey. What separates a hero from the other characters in the story? It isn't that they never suffer or fail, but rather that they never give up on what they believe in.

When our heroes doubt their own abilities, make mistakes, learn painful lessons, reach rock bottom, and are misunderstood by those around them, we see them as inspiring, brave, and strong. How would it feel to extend that same empathy and grace to yourself—to recognize yourself as the hero of your story? Spend some time journaling your thoughts about this topic or perhaps even writing a short story or creating artwork that tells the tale of your hero's journey. Let yourself feel proud, inspired, and appreciative of your own strength.

Connect and Gather

When you carry the witch wound, one of the most healing steps you can take is to connect with other people who experience the world like you. According to a 2017 Pew Research Center report, 27 percent of American adults think of themselves as spiritual but not religious.[1] The number of self-identified witches, pagans, druids, herbalists, energy healers, tarot readers, and psychics is on the rise too—not just in the United States, but globally.

Today, most midsize and major cities have Facebook groups where spiritual and magical individuals can interact. Searching for hashtags like #witchcraft and #spiritualhealing on Instagram will yield millions of posts from practitioners around the world. And countless witches and spiritual leaders have formed covens, healing circles, and other in-person groups. Whether you do so online or within your local community, connecting with like-minded souls can help you realize that you are not alone and millions of people think like you do. These communities can serve as safe spaces to practice letting yourself be seen and held. It can be deeply healing to connect, learn together, and feel supported in these spaces.

While connecting and gathering are important for spiritual individuals of all genders, it can feel especially validating for women who carry the memory of social restriction in their bodies and psyches. Remember the 1547 proclamation that forbade English women from gathering to "babble and talk" and instructed men to keep their wives inside the home? Search for women's groups and healing circles online or in your local area; they are popping up more and more frequently in cities all around the world. If there isn't one near you, consider starting a group of your own. Gathering with a few of your closest friends every full moon to "babble and talk," bake cookies, and drink wine most certainly counts.

Lastly, building relationships and relying on other people in your community for support is yet another way to revolt against patriarchy, capitalism, and imperialism. Collaboration and interdependence are deeply destabilizing to a society that encourages individualism, competition, and domination of resources. Do with that wisdom what you will!

RITUAL FOR CREATING AN EMPOWERMENT SIGIL

A sigil is a symbol that has been charged with magical intention. Sigil magic enables the practitioner to gain clarity about their intentions and manifest their desired outcome. Some witches believe that working with sigils allows them to communicate with their subconscious mind or highest self to create change on an inner level, while others use sigils to make their intention known to the spirits they work with or even to the universe itself. In any case, sigil magic is all about cocreating your own reality.

If you carry the witch wound, creating your own empowerment sigil can help you reclaim and stay rooted in your personal power, break through mental blocks, and boost your confidence.

Timing: Perform this ritual when the moon is in the waxing phase.

Location: Anywhere.

Tools: You will need a pen and a piece of paper.

Before beginning the ritual, make any additional preparations you prefer—such as dimming the lights, playing meditative music, or lighting candles.

Then, energetically cleanse and bless your ritual space using your preferred method—such as burning incense, ringing a bell, or drawing out negative energy with a crystal. If you do not have any energy-cleansing tools available, you may visualize and sense a white ball of light glowing inside your solar plexus and expanding outward into a protective white sphere. Whichever method you use, state your intention to cleanse and protect your ritual space, thereby making it sacred and separating it from the mundane world.

When you are ready, open the ritual by taking a comfortable seat of your choice. Close your eyes and take three deep, slow inhales and exhales, inviting your physical body to relax and any mental chatter to fade away.

Allow your learnings and realizations about the witch wound to bubble up from the cauldron of your soul. Reflect on how this wound has impacted your beliefs, behaviors, and experiences throughout your life. Gradually, allow your thoughts to drift toward the path of healing. Consider your greatest dreams and ambitions, as well as the blocks and obstacles you must first overcome to reach those goals.

Let these reflections guide you toward one intention that can be summarized into a succinct phrase. You may choose to begin this phrase with "I am" or "I have," or you can simply describe your desired outcome. Examples include "I live my truth" or "confidence in all situations." Be sure to narrow your focus down to just one intention. You can always repeat this ritual to create more sigils, but each one should be precise. Additionally, your intention should only include positive terms, avoiding the use of negative words such as *don't* or *won't,* and should be phrased as if it is already happening now. For example, "I am infinitely creative" is a stronger intention than "I will become more creative" or "I am not creatively blocked anymore."

Write your intention down on the piece of paper. Now, cross out every vowel and every repeating letter. For example, if your original intention was "confidence in all situations" you would be left with the letters *c n f d l s t.* From here, you will need to conjure your creative abilities to help you design a sigil using these remaining letters. Let your imagination run wild—flip letters backward or upside down, shrink some letters and enlarge others, or fit one letter inside another. Feel free to add your own artistic flair. At the end, you should have one symbol made from the connecting curves and lines of the letters.

Finally, you must charge your sigil. Allow yourself to sink into a meditative state as you gaze upon your sigil. If you like, you can use your mind's eye to travel down the spiral staircase to the personal place of power you discovered in chapter 10's full moon ritual and continue with the remainder of this ritual there. In either case, repeat your intention over and over, either aloud or in your mind, as you focus on the sigil. You may also trace the sigil repeatedly with your index finger. The goal is to allow your sigil to become embedded in your subconscious mind. Playing rhythmic music, dancing, drumming, or chanting can assist with this. There are many ways to charge a sigil, and over time you may find alternative methods that work best for you.

When you intuitively feel that your sigil has been sufficiently charged, fold up the piece of paper so the sigil is concealed, and hide the paper away in a safe place. Resist the urge to look at your sigil in the future; the idea is to allow your conscious mind to fully release the sigil to your subconscious mind. Some witches even prefer to burn their sigils when they are done creating them. You may do so using a fireproof dish, if this method feels right to you.

It has been said that if you want something you have never had, you must be willing to do something you have never done. What is something you have never done in the name of self-empowerment? Trusting in your own creativity and talent? Letting others see the real you? Taking a risk on your dreams? Believing in magic? Are you willing to give these things a try?

You are the hero of your story. *You are enough*, exactly as you are. Let this truth be the source of your empowerment and guide you in all that you do.

12

Ancestral Healing

When you heal the witch wound in yourself, you also help to heal the people in your inner circle, the community at large, your descendants, and even your ancestors—those who came before you who no longer exist in this realm. When your ancestors passed on, many of them left behind unfinished business and unhealed traumas. Some of these wounds may have continued to be passed down and left untended, until *you* eventually inherited them. By stopping the cycle of trauma here and now, you help those who came before you find peace in the otherworld.

Of course, none of us knows for certain what awaits us on the other side of the veil—the one that separates our mundane, physical world from the spiritual realm of the dead beyond. Perhaps you are not even sure if you believe in the existence of such a realm at all. Personally, I do—very much so. Ancestor veneration is an important part of my spiritual practice and has been for years. When I find myself in my darkest hours, my ancestors are the ones I turn to first. They are the ones I can always trust to answer my prayers and deliver comfort in times of need.

Ancestral healing can be an important part of tending the witch wound, especially if you sense patterns of behaviors or beliefs related to this wound in your family line. As someone doing ancestral healing work, you are the bridge between worlds—the dead and the living, the past and the future. This work can take the form of honoring your spiritual heritage, connecting with your well and wise ancestors, healing your wounded ancestors, and breaking the cycle of inherited trauma in your lineage.

Reconnecting to Your Spiritual Heritage

How much do you know about the spiritual beliefs and traditions of your ancestors? Not just your grandparents or great-grandparents, but your ancient ancestors—the ones who walked this Earth thousands of years ago? Do you know the names of the gods and goddesses they worshipped? Do you know the plants they viewed as sacred and used as medicine? Do you know the kinds of rituals they held, the myths and legends they passed down orally, and the holy sites they visited?

For me, discovering the answers to these questions about my own ancestors was life-altering. Though I have always thought of myself as a spiritual person and began exploring witchcraft at a young age, for much of my life I felt a bit adrift in my spirituality—as if I never quite fit in anywhere. Like many others, I was primarily drawn to New Age spirituality during the early years of my journey. But as I would later learn, many of the practices and tools that have been labeled "New Age" are actually sacred traditions belonging to Asian and Indigenous American cultures that have been stripped-down and repackaged to appeal to white, Western consumers.

This, of course, is a form of cultural appropriation—the act of adopting customs, practices, symbols, or other elements of a culture to which one does not belong in a way that does not respect their original meaning or context. One common example of cultural appropriation in New Age spirituality is when non-Indigenous vendors sell tools like white sage smudge sticks and dream catchers without learning about or explaining the true sacred symbolism behind these practices. Another example is when someone displays a statue of the Buddha in their home purely for aesthetics without practicing Buddhism or adhering to the religion's rules about how to respectfully position the statue.

Whether you are visiting your local occult shop or browsing spiritual hashtags online, it is impossible to avoid these commonly appropriated symbols, traditions, and practices. They are accepted and supported by the spiritual community at large—but that does not make them right. Certainly, no witch or spiritual individual engages in cultural appropriation because they desire to cause harm to other people and cultures. Rather, they feel called to get in touch with Spirit and to bring deeper meaning and magic into their worlds. New Age spirituality is one of the most accessible gateways to this calling. Yet the intention behind our actions is less important than their impact—and many Indigenous, Asian, Black, and other people of color have been harmed by cultural appropriation in spirituality. Once we become aware of this truth, all of us have a responsibility to do better.

The thing is, we also all have ancestors who were indigenous to *somewhere*. We all descend from people who had rich cultural and spiritual traditions that were passed down through generations, who were deeply connected to the Earth and the rhythms of nature—including those of us with European ancestry. Sadly, many of the stories and customs from pre-Christian European cultures were lost centuries ago when those ancestors converted to Christianity. For individuals like myself who were born in the United States, there is an additional degree of separation.

Yet thanks to the combined efforts of archaeologists, historians, linguists, professors, authors, and religious reconstructionists, those of us with European ancestry do know some key things about the spiritual beliefs of our ancient ancestors. For instance, we know their spirituality was deeply ingrained with every aspect of their lives, from farming and hunting to war, childbirth, and death. We also know they worshipped in groves, near bogs and lakes, on hills and mountaintops—that these wild places were spiritual, powerful, and magical to them. And we know they were polytheists who worshipped many gods and goddesses, along with land spirits and ancestral spirits.

Learning about the old ways of my own ancestors—who lived in Denmark, Sweden, Germany, Ireland, England, and elsewhere in Northern Europe—is what led me to my spiritual path: Nordic paganism, with heavy influences from Druidry. While both Norse paganism and Druidry are open traditions that can be practiced by anyone regardless of their heritage or ethnicity, I personally find deep meaning in celebrating the same festivals, venerating the same deities, and studying the same esoteric arts as my ancient ancestors.

Similarly, my approach to witchcraft has been shaped by folklore and practices from these regions. Much of what I do falls under the umbrella of *seiðr* or Norse magic, including spirit flight, *galdr* (singing incantations), and runic divination. I also incorporate elements of folk magic from the various other places where my ancestors lived, including Germany and England. Some of the knowledge of these practices actually derives from trial records during the Burning Times.

Coming home to paganism and witchcraft has played a vital role in healing my witch wound and stopping the cycle of inherited trauma. By reclaiming your ancestral practices instead of appropriating the sacred traditions of Indigenous cultures, you embody the legacy of your well and wise ancestors rather than your wounded ancestors. Thus, you begin to heal the witch wound–adjacent harms of colonialism, capitalism, and patriarchy in your family line.

It's important to note that you can do this work even if you are adopted or do not know your cultural or ethnic background. In fact, it's quite simple—not always easy, but simple. All that is required of you is to ask your ancestors to show you where you come from, listen for their answers, and trust what you discover through visions, dreams, synchronicities, or feelings.

Surprisingly, it's not the asking or the listening that is difficult for most people—it's the trusting. Again, this goes back to believing that our intuition is inherently flawed, dangerous, or worthless. For the sake of this exercise, do your best to let your walls down and remain open to whatever wisdom comes through. If it helps, start by approaching this work with the mindset of "I'm going to *pretend* everything I learn is real and true." As you become more comfortable with leaning on your psychic and intuitive insights, this work will become easier.

Reigniting Ancestral Traditions

One of the things that separates modern people from our ancient ancestors is the art of oral storytelling and passing down of spiritual and cultural customs. In many families this practice died out during the Burning Times, when it became unsafe to align oneself too closely with the old pagan ways. That said, there is nothing stopping you from reigniting this custom in your own family—and remember, chosen family is family too.

You can do this by inviting your trusted loved ones to participate in your spiritual and cultural practices. If you are a pagan witch, tell your children stories about the origins of holidays like Samhain and write down your rituals and spells to leave behind for future generations. If you are a tarot reader, offer to do readings for your friends or even lead a small informal workshop. If you are an herbalist, give your herbal teas and infusions to your loved ones and teach them about the healing properties of each plant. Host an annual Yule party; invite friends to gather for a bonfire every new moon; or start an entirely new tradition in your inner circle.

Gathering, sharing, and passing down cultural and spiritual traditions is a time-honored practice that our ancestors upheld for tens of thousands of years. By reigniting this custom, you repattern your nervous system to accept that this behavior is safe and sacred.

Creating an Ancestor Altar

Ancestor veneration is the practice of holding remembrance and reverence for those who came before you. Creating a simple ancestor altar and praying to your well and wise ancestors for support and guidance are wonderful ways to begin this work.

All you need is a flat surface where you can arrange a few items, such as the top of a dresser, a shelf, or a windowsill. This space will function as your ancestor altar. Decorate it with anything and everything that reminds you of your ancestors and your beloved dead—photos, memorabilia, family heirlooms, country flags, your family tree, crystals, candles, herbs, and more.

Visit your ancestor altar regularly to show remembrance and respect to those who came before you, whose stories are still alive in your blood and bones. If ancestor veneration is new to you, start by simply saying hello! Your ancestors are already there for you and they want to be contacted, so don't feel like you need to be too formal or structured. I like to visit my ancestor altar at least once a week to give offerings (fresh clean water is a beautiful free offering) but also to simply spend time speaking with my ancestors and letting them know that I love them, I remember them, and I respect them.

Reflections for Ancestral Remembrance

These reflection questions are designed to guide you through an exploration of your cultural and spiritual ancestry. You may not know the answers to some or all of these questions, and that is perfectly fine. The idea is not to get all of the answers right, but rather to open yourself to the wisdom of your ancestors. If a particular topic sparks your interest, by all means, use books or the internet to descend deep into research and learning. But don't be afraid to retreat inward in your quest for wisdom; to sink down into the depths of your own knowing and drink in the answers that flow from your inner cauldron of wisdom, for this cauldron is tended by your ancestors. Let these stories visit you in your dreams, visions, and meditations.

1. What lands did your ancestors live on? What did they call these lands, and what are these lands called now?

2. What languages did your ancestors speak?

3. What landforms, bodies of water, trees, plants, stones, and other geographical features were important to your ancestors?

4. How did your ancestors acknowledge or celebrate the rhythms of nature—the changing of the seasons, the tides, the moon phases?

5. What magical traditions did your ancestors uphold? What folklore inspired these practices?

6. What deities did your ancestors believe in? How did they worship them?

7. What foods did your ancestors eat?

8. What rites of passage did your ancestors practice? (Birth, coming of age, marriage, death, etc.)

9. What did your ancestors believe happened to the soul after death?

10. What are the origin and history of your surname?

ANCESTRAL HEALING RITUAL

This is a powerful ritual for connecting with your well and wise ancestors, liberating yourself from inherited trauma, and clearing old programming on both a soul level and a DNA level. Ancestor work can be quite emotional, so do your best to make sure you won't be interrupted during the ritual and give yourself ample time to reflect and process afterward.

Timing: Anytime.

Location: Anywhere.

Tools: You will need a white candle, a black candle, two candle-holders, a lighter, a pen, a scrap of paper, tongs or tweezers for handling burning paper, and a firesafe dish.

Before beginning the ritual, make any additional preparations you prefer—such as dimming the lights, playing meditative music, or lighting candles.

Then, energetically cleanse and bless your ritual space using your preferred method—such as burning incense, ringing a bell, or drawing out negative energy with a crystal. If you do not have any energy-cleansing tools available, you may visualize and sense a white ball of light glowing inside your solar plexus and expanding outward into a protective white sphere. Whichever method you use, state your intention to cleanse and protect your ritual space, thereby making it sacred and separating it from the mundane world.

When you are ready, speak the following words aloud:

"Ancestors of blood and bone, who gave life to my body; ancestors of heart, who were dear to me in life and have passed from this world; ancestors of spirit, who inspire me with the paths you paved and the wisdom you shared—I greet you and welcome you into this sacred space."

The next part of the ritual involves stating your name and reciting your known genealogy, beginning with your parents and working up your family tree to your grandparents, great-grandparents, and so on. Recite the names of as many ancestors as you know or can remember. If you are adopted, you may choose to honor your biological family's ancestors, adoptive family's ancestors, or both. Use this format:

"I am [state your name],
Daughter/son/child of [first parent's name] and [second parent's name],
Granddaughter/grandson/grandchild of [list all known grandparents' names],
Great-granddaughter/grandson/grandchild of [list all known great-grandparents' names] . . ."

If you do not know the names of one or more parents or ancestors, or if there are specific ancestors you do not wish to honor, it is perfectly fine to omit those names. Stating your own name aloud is the most important part of this ritual. Your well and wise ancestral spirits will recognize you even if you do not know their names.

Now, speak the following words out loud:

"Well and wise ancestors near and far, stretching back into the reaches of time, I call out to you now. I remember you; I honor you; and I thank you for every challenge you endured, every sacrifice you made, and every path you followed that led to my existence. This candle burns in your memory."

Light the white candle. If it feels right, spend a few moments feeling yourself surrounded, supported, and held by your well and wise ancestors.

Next, take your black candle and light it by touching the wick to the white candle's flame. This act is symbolic of the passing of the ancestral torch. Imagine that this second candle is imbued with the ancient wisdom, love, and protection of your well and wise ancestors.

Now, spend a moment reflecting on a limiting belief or fear you hold, such as "I will be rejected if I show my true self" or "the world is an unsafe place to exist." Is it possible that this limiting belief stems from one or more of your ancestors and has been passed down to you?

Reflect on your known ancestors and the lives they lived, as well as the lives you think your unknown ancestors may have lived. Of course, you don't know every ancestor's story—if you have identified a limiting belief that feels like it may be an ancestral wound, even if you are not sure, trust that instinct.

Write this limiting belief down on a small piece of paper. Feel into the idea that this belief did not originate within you, but was passed down to you through your DNA and family conditioning. Understand that this burden is not yours to carry and that you have the power to release it and break the cycle. As you reflect on this truth, speak the following words:

"This belief is not mine, and I release it with ease."

Repeat the above words as many times as feels appropriate to you. Then, using your tongs or tweezers, hold the paper to the black candle's flame and light it on fire. Imagine the flames burning away this harmful limiting belief, cleansing it from your body, mind, and spirit. Allow the paper to burn down in the fireproof dish, relighting as needed. Dispose of the ashes after they have cooled.

By calling your ancestors into the work of healing the witch wound, you break the cycle of shame and suffering that has been passed down to you through your DNA and bring peace to those who are gone from this world. Of course, we all have ancestors we would rather not honor or connect with. This might include relatives who were abusive in life or distant ancestors who were bigoted, racist, sexist, homophobic, or violent. You can exclude these ancestors by using a phrase such as "I call upon my well and wise ancestors who have my best interests at heart." You can also cast a circle or sphere of protection (as you learned in chapter 10) and state that only your well and wise ancestors may enter your sacred space.

13

Healing the Divine
Feminine

In chapter 9, we discussed our planet's imbalance of Divine Feminine and Divine Masculine energies. It is important to note that on the grand scale of human history, this is a relatively new phenomenon; things were not always this way. For the majority of human existence, women were not only viewed as more or less equal to men, but their unique gifts and abilities were *celebrated* rather than shamed.

A growing number of historians, archaeologists, and anthropologists agree that gender inequality is a relatively recent development in human history, beginning roughly twelve thousand years ago at the end of the Paleolithic era. In the nearly 290,000 years leading up to this turning point (based on the fossil evidence that the earliest modern humans lived 300,000 years ago[1]), women contributed greatly to the well-being and survival of their communities, and gender-based division of labor was largely flexible. For hundreds of thousands of years, all members of the community were taught the skills that were essential for survival, primarily gathering and hunting. Indeed, this may have been the most gender-equal time in all of human history.[2]

Yet there is also evidence that women were highly regarded and celebrated in ways that were distinct from men—namely for their ability to birth life into the world, which these ancient cultures may have viewed as a divine connection to the otherworld. It was during the Paleolithic era that the religious beliefs and practices categorized as "shamanic" developed in Northern Europe and Asia. In fact, the earliest known artistic representation of a shaman is a carved ivory figure in the shape of a female head.[3] This carving was discovered near the burial site of a woman who died when she was around forty years old. She would have been considered an elder in her time, meaning she would have been revered for her wisdom and wielded great influence in her community.

Another carving, known as the Venus of Dolní Věstonice, was discovered at the same archaeological site. This is one of more than two hundred Venus figurines that have been unearthed throughout Europe and Asia, the most famous being the Venus of Willendorf. Despite these types of figures being carved over a period of twenty thousand years, all share certain striking similarities: they each have small faceless heads, wide hips and thighs, large breasts and bellies, and prominent vulvae. These mysterious figurines have been interpreted as symbols of female sexuality and fertility, a primordial mother goddess, or perhaps even a supreme female creator.[4]

For women living in the modern era, the realities of the far distant past can be difficult to imagine. How is it possible that the female body—milk-filled breasts, round pregnant bellies, wide birthing hips, proudly displayed labia—was celebrated and even worshipped tens of thousands of years ago, when women today are shamed simply for breastfeeding their children in public? How is it possible that a woman who lived thirty thousand years ago could have been regarded as a religious leader and influential decision-maker, when female leaders today are reduced to their physical appearances and toxic gender stereotypes?

According to some scholars, women's status in society first began to decline with the adoption of agriculture around twelve thousand years ago, at the start of the Neolithic era.[5] As humans began to build permanent settlements and acquire more resources, it became necessary to defend against possible invaders. The members of society who were physically strongest and most aggressive—usually men—were tasked with protecting the community. Subsequently, women began spending less time outside the home gathering resources and more time inside the home tending to children and domestic tasks. Of course, Neolithic religions still largely centered around goddess worship; while women's roles and status had begun to shift, the wisdom of the Sacred Feminine was still very much alive.

It was not until the Christianization of Europe, which occurred during the last two thousand years, that the last remnants of these ancient, ancestral, Earth-based spiritual beliefs and practices were wiped out. The divine connection between women and the rhythms of nature—the menstrual cycle, the lunar phases, the eternal cycle of life and death—was lost. The spiritual significance of the female body was not only forgotten, but violently erased. Organized religion, patriarchy, and colonialism worked hand in hand to conquer the world and grow the influence of men, stripping women of their unique power in the process. During the Burning Times, those women who fought back were silenced forever.

This leads us to today. While the world is no doubt a difficult place to exist in a female body, we cannot ignore the reality that many women today have certain rights and freedoms that our female ancestors from five hundred years ago could only have dreamed about. As an American, I am free to express my magic, my witchiness, and my sensuality without the risk of being sentenced to death. While societal norms and personal insecurities often make this difficult, the fact stands: under the law, I am free to reclaim and reconnect with the Divine Feminine wisdom of ancient times.

Reflecting on the above truths—that our species once had deep reverence for the sacred magic of women, that all but a few traces of that reverence have been lost to time and history, and that I am now free to reclaim and revive that sanctity—pains my heart, but also fills me with immense hope and a sense of connection to my feminine ancestors who walked this Earth.

While healing the Divine Feminine can be especially important for modern women, it is beneficial for people of all genders, as well as for society as a collective. In the pages that follow, you will find exercises, rituals, and ideas to help you heal your relationship with the Divine Feminine. These practices are not exclusive to any one gender or sex, though they may resonate most deeply for individuals who feel—or want to feel—connected to their feminine energy. The one exception is a section that focuses on the menstrual cycle, which was written for people who menstruate and who desire a more spiritual connection with their monthly bleed.

Honor Your Embodiment of the Divine Feminine

Intuition, sensitivity, creativity, empathy, compassion, sensuality—while people of all genders can and do possess these qualities, in many spiritual traditions these traits are linked with the Divine Feminine. Tragically, these characteristics are not widely valued or rewarded in our patriarchal, capitalist society—especially compared to traits traditionally associated with the Divine Masculine such as strength, logic, action, courage, and responsibility.

But this doesn't mean *you* can't value and celebrate these qualities. One way to do this is by holding a ritual to celebrate your embodiment of the Divine Feminine. After energetically cleansing and blessing your ritual space, light a white candle and speak aloud those feminine qualities you love and cherish most about yourself while gazing into the flame. Additionally, think about ways you can nurture your own embodiment of the Divine Feminine, such as learning a new creative skill simply for the pleasure and joy of it—rather than with the goal of mastering it or turning it into a source of income.

Embody the Feminine Archetypes

The Swiss psychoanalyst Carl Jung is famed for his work in developing the concept of archetypes—images and themes that are recurring and universal. Jung believed these archetypes originated in the collective unconscious and were identifiable in myths, legends, songs, and artwork throughout history and around the globe. Over the years, numerous Jungian analysts and psychiatrists have identified and developed various other archetypes. Some are gender-neutral, while others represent aspects of the masculine or feminine.

Below are a few of the most well-known feminine archetypes and what they symbolize:

- The Maiden: Youth, innocence, learning, wonder, curiosity

- The Mother: Fertility, creation, compassion, generosity, nurturing

- The Crone: Wisdom, maturity, introspection, patience, inner peace

- The Queen: Leadership, power, confidence, loyalty, partnership

- The Huntress: Fearlessness, independence, freedom, self-reliance, ambition

- The Lover: Sensuality, passion, pleasure, magnetism, creativity

- The Mystic: Intuition, imagination, spirituality, healing, mystery

Everyone can practice embodying these feminine archetypes and use them to navigate challenging situations or generate positive changes in their lives. For instance, if you are working on a big creative project such as an art portfolio or a book, you might embody the Mother archetype to tap into the energy of creation and metaphorically birth your idea into being. The Maiden can be a wonderful archetype to embody when you are learning a new skill; she approaches new experiences with open-mindedness and enthusiasm and isn't afraid to make mistakes.

If you are feeling bogged down by the stresses of life, connecting with the energy of the Lover can remind you to play, dance, create, and find the joy of each moment. And when you need to drum up courage to speak your truth in a difficult moment or take a leap of faith on a new career or endeavor, you can't go wrong by embodying the energy of the Huntress.

Learning about, connecting with, and embodying these feminine archetypes are powerful ways to open your own heart to the beauty and magic of the Divine Feminine and activate this energy on a global scale.

Prioritize Your Rest

If there is one thing our modern capitalist society abhors, it is rest. From the time we are born, we are conditioned to believe that rest is something we must earn; rest is something we only deserve once we have accomplished enough and produced enough. This is a lie! The truth is that rest is a basic, Earth-given right that belongs to everyone. Prioritizing your own rest is a beautiful way to fight against this capitalist conditioning—driven by an overabundance of masculine, action-oriented energy—and embrace the gentle, receptive energy of the Sacred Feminine.

Do you often feel exhausted, burned out, and stretched thin as a result of this go, go, go lifestyle? I certainly do. For the longest time, I simply believed that I was lazy. What other reason could explain why I was seemingly never able to keep up; never able to do, produce, earn, and achieve as much as the people around me? As I became more embodied and tuned in to my needs and trauma responses, I realized that I wasn't lazy: my nervous system simply required more rest than I had been allowing myself to have. I wasn't the problem; my capitalist conditioning was.

Embracing the spirit of rest has been deeply healing to my nervous system and physical body, but has also done wonders for my self-worth and overall life satisfaction. What's more, I have discovered that when I give myself space to properly rest and rejuvenate, I am able to do my best creative work.

Heal the Witch Wound

Start by devoting a set block of time one night per week to pure rest and relaxation. I have chosen Thursday nights myself between seven and nine o'clock in the evening as my weekly "me-time." This is not to say that I don't rest during other times of the week, but rather that these two hours are a sacred block of rest time that I never miss, no matter how busy the week gets. If you can only snag twenty minutes, do that! Silence your phone and set it aside to minimize potential distractions, and then spend that time simply delighting in the bliss of rest.

Read, watch your favorite feel-good movie, do a puzzle, or drink a cup of tea and enjoy the ambience of your home or backyard. If you notice something that needs to be taken care of, like crumbs on the counter or a messy couch, give yourself permission to let it go until your time of rest is done. Notice how good it feels to simply exist without needing to do anything in particular. Regular meditation, self-reflection, and moments of stillness and quiet are likewise important in activating and healing Divine Feminine energy.

Start a Self-Love Journal

You can start a new journal specifically for this work, or you can use an existing journal. Each morning or evening, write down three things you love about yourself. Think about personality traits, quirks, skills, body parts, physical characteristics, and other qualities. It is perfectly fine to include some things that position you relative to other people—such as being a devoted parent or a valuable employee—but make sure you also acknowledge qualities that do not center around producing or providing for other people.

Perhaps you love that you have a curious mind or that you are able to find joy in the little moments like steeping a cup of tea. For me, this work was especially powerful in healing my relationship with my body. I remember feeling genuine love and tenderness for body parts that had once made me ashamed and frustrated, like my belly and my thighs, because I realized all they had enabled me to do and experience. This is a simple exercise, yet one that can be profoundly healing.

Support the Global Feminist Movement

Over the past century or so, the women's rights movement has made tremendous strides toward gender equality. Yet there is still much work to be done when it comes to leveling the playing field between all genders and protecting women from sexual assault, domestic violence, and discrimination.

Educating yourself about women's issues, donating time or money to women's organizations (including local women's shelters and clinics that provide access to reproductive care), participating in women's marches and rallies, writing to elected officials, and voting with both your ballot and your dollars are all effective ways to support the global feminist movement and to heal the planetary imbalance of Divine Feminine energy.

Celebrate Female Friendships

During the Burning Times, female friendships were a dangerous thing. After being subjected to days—or in some cases, weeks and even months—of imprisonment and horrific torture, many accused witches named their fellow women as accomplices in their supposed "malicious schemes." Daughters accused mothers; sisters accused sisters. Today, this wound shows up in the form of women mistrusting other women or feeling threatened by other women's success, beauty, wealth, or happiness.

One way to heal this symptom of the witch wound is by celebrating, honoring, and nurturing the healthy relationships you have with the women in your life: mothers, daughters, sisters, grandmothers, aunts, cousins, and friends. Take advantage of every opportunity to uplift the women around you. Open your heart to them and encourage them to do the same. Tell them they are capable, intelligent, strong, beautiful, courageous, and important. Hold space for them during their difficult moments, and most importantly, be their most vocal supporter during their moments of accomplishment and joy.

Connect with Your Menstrual Cycle

If you are someone who bleeds each month, you have a powerful opportunity to embody the Divine Feminine by connecting more deeply with your menstrual cycle. One way to do this is by noticing how your menstrual cycle is reflective of the rhythms and cycles of nature on a grand scale—as within, so without. You can think of your cycle in terms of either inner moons or inner seasons, depending on which imagery resonates most.

First, it's worth noting that the words *month*, *moon*, and *menstruation* all share common etymology. The modern English word *moon* is derived from the Proto-Germanic *menon*, which evolved into the Old English *mona*. Similarly, the word *month* is derived from the Proto-Germanic *menoth* and the Old English *monað*. Why are the old terms for *moon* and *month* so similar? It stems from how humans used the lunar cycle to track the passage of time before our current calendar system was developed. One month corresponded with one lunar cycle, from new moon to new moon—a period of twenty-nine days.

In Latin, the term for *month* was *mensis*, which gives us the origin of the English words *menses* and *menstruation*. In Old English, this was known as *monaðblot*, or "month-blood." It's not difficult to see how this linguistic connection was made: the average menstrual cycle is twenty-eight days (though cycles can range from twenty-one to thirty-six days)—roughly the same as that of one lunar cycle. Many ancient peoples, such as the Greeks, believed that the monthly lunar and menstrual cycles were linked. Thus, many people who bleed like to think of their inner cycle in terms of the phases of the moon:

- New Moon (Menstruation): Rest, introspection, solitude, release

- Waxing Moon (Follicular Phase): Growth, creativity, problem-solving

- Full Moon (Ovulation): Celebration, confidence, peak energy

- Waning Moon (Luteal Phase): Winding down, reflection, sensitivity

From these descriptions, you might notice that the menstrual cycle mirrors yet another cycle from the natural world: that of the seasons. In this context, menstruation is associated with winter; the follicular (pre-ovulation) phase is linked with spring; ovulation represents summer; and the luteal (premenstrual) phase is paired with autumn.

Thinking about your cycle in terms of either seasons or lunar phases can help you become more present and tuned in to the needs of your body at each stage of your cycle—a deeply healing act for your inner Divine Feminine. For instance, you might discover that you have a lower capacity for dealing with highly stimulating environments during your inner new moon/inner winter. Knowing this, you may choose to avoid scheduling important meetings or committing to social plans during your bleed.

Most people today treat menstruation as an inconvenience at best, or something dirty and shameful at worst. Again, these are lies taught to us by patriarchy and capitalism. Your menstrual cycle is sacred and magical. By nurturing your relationship with your monthly rhythms, you can honor your inner Divine Feminine and unlock deeper awareness and connection with your body, your mood, and your energy levels.

DIVINE FEMININE RITUAL BATH

The Divine Feminine is associated with qualities such as creativity, compassion, gentleness, receptiveness, intuition, empathy, and sensuality. In various spiritual and esoteric traditions, both the moon and the element of water are linked with these same attributes. For this reason, preparing a ritual bath—or shower—on the night of the full moon is a powerful way to connect with and embody the spirit of the Divine Feminine and to support intentions of self-love. Water is also physically and energetically purifying; when combined with the power of the full moon, this ritual has the potential to be deeply healing for your wounded inner witch.

Timing: Perform this ritual on the full moon, ideally at night after the sun has set and the moon has risen.

Location: Perform this ritual in your bathtub or shower.

Tools: You will need one cup of pink Himalayan salt and a handful of rose petals to add to your bathwater. You may also add any other botanicals or essential oils that you associate with the Divine Feminine. If you are taking a ritual shower instead of a bath, use a Himalayan salt scrub (store-bought or homemade) and a rose-scented shower steamer instead. If you have them, I also recommend using rose quartz and moonstone crystals in this ritual.

Before preparing your ritual bath, make any additional preparations you prefer—such as dimming the lights, playing meditative music, or lighting candles.

Then, energetically cleanse and bless your space using your preferred method—such as burning incense, ringing a bell, or drawing out negative energy with a crystal. If you do not have any energy-cleansing tools available, you may visualize and sense a white ball of light glowing inside your solar plexus and expanding outward into a protective white sphere. Whichever method you use, state your intention to cleanse and protect your ritual space, thereby making it sacred and separating it from the mundane world.

When you are ready, turn on the faucet and allow your bathtub to fill with water. As you wait for it to fill, visualize the full moon glowing with silvery-white light in the sky above you. Imagine this light penetrating through the roof and walls of your home, shining down into the tub as it fills with water. Feel the moon's light purifying your bathwater and blessing it with pure lunar energy. (If you are preparing a ritual shower rather than a bath, perform this same visualization while waiting for the water to warm up. Sense the moon's light purifying and blessing each droplet of water as it falls from your showerhead.)

At this point, add your pink Himalayan salt and rose petals to your bathwater. If you have rose quartz or moonstone crystals available, place these on the edge of the tub. Using your hand, gently stir the bathwater in a clockwise direction and speak one of the following intentions out loud three times:

"The healing power of the Divine Feminine flows through every cell of my body."

"My heart is open to giving and receiving infinite amounts of love."

"Receiving pleasure is my sacred birthright, and I receive it with ease."

"My body is a divine gift, and I treat it with love and kindness."

"I am learning to love myself more and more every day."

"Creativity flows through me in abundance."

Your bathwater is now charged with your magical healing intention; sense it radiating with Divine Feminine energy. Carefully lower yourself into the tub, allowing as much of your body to become submerged as you are comfortable with.

If you are preparing a ritual shower instead, speak your chosen intention after getting into the shower, while gentling applying your pink Himalayan salt scrub in a clockwise motion over all parts of your body. Sense that the salt scrub is infused with the energy of your healing intention and the Divine Feminine as you apply it.

Spend as much time as you desire soaking in your ritual bath or enjoying your ritual shower, feeling the water around you vibrating with healing energy. Gentle, loving self-touch on any parts of the body that you feel require extra attention and healing can go a long way toward amplifying the effects of this ritual.

Heal the Witch Wound

For many women, healing their inner wounded feminine and embodying the Divine Feminine may prove to be one of the most profound steps they can take to heal the witch wound. Of course, men and nonbinary individuals can benefit from this kind of healing work as well. Regardless of your gender, I hope you have taken something meaningful away from this chapter: that you are deeply deserving of self-love and compassion, of rest, and of existing for a purpose simpler yet simultaneously more sacred and fulfilling than endlessly working, producing, and earning. This is what it means to embrace and embody the Divine Feminine.

14

Somatic Healing

The witch wound is much more than a set of fears and insecurities that live within your mind; it is a physiological trauma response that is triggered by the nervous system. This trauma response can be passed down to you through your DNA or established through cultural conditioning. That is why you can literally *feel* the witch wound being activated within your energetic and physical body.

It's also why your body is one of the most important allies you have. I say *ally*, because whether you believe in the concept of a soul or not, you are in many ways *not* your body. Rather, you are the one who exists *within* your body—the consciousness who observes it, responds to it, and cares for it. This is not to say the body isn't spiritual. Quite the opposite! As you progress in your journey to heal the witch wound, it is important to explore, deepen, and nurture your relationship with your own body.

Certainly, caring for your physical health and developing a positive body image are important components of this. But even more vital is learning how to *listen* to your body, and then *respond* to those insights, clues, and requests. You may be surprised to discover the deep mysteries your body is able to share with you through this sacred work.

Create a Foundation of Safety

Creating a foundation of safety and stability within your own body is one of the most important steps you can take to heal the witch wound. When your body is stuck in fight-or-flight mode—in other words, when you walk around in a constant state of anxiety and hypervigilance, as those of us who carry the witch wound often do—the body uses a large percentage of its own energy to simply stay alert and stay alive. In this state, you have minimal leftover mental, emotional, spiritual, and physical capacity for diving deep into the work of healing the witch wound. By comparison, a regulated nervous system has a higher capacity to tolerate uncomfortable emotions and sensations—such as those associated with speaking your truth or being seen in your magic.

For this work, I cannot recommend strongly enough that you lean on the support and guidance of a trained professional, if you have the resources to do so.[1] Somatic experiencing, cognitive behavioral therapy, EMDR (eye movement desensitization and reprocessing), EFT (emotional freedom technique), dance or movement therapy, and other forms of therapy are all wonderful tools that can help you untangle yourself from your thoughts and become more embodied and present.

For many people—whether due to financial barriers or geographical ones—working with a qualified therapist or clinician is not an option. Fortunately, you can begin the process of building a foundation of safety in your body and mind with a simple somatic awareness exercise. Try it right now: keeping your eyes open and your breath natural, sit quietly and slowly scan your body from your feet all the way to the top of your head. Do not rush this. Notice how each toe feels before moving onto the ball of your foot, then the ankle, the calf, the knee, the front of the thigh, the back of the thigh, upward into the hip and groin, and so on.

Which body parts feel tight, tense, constricted, or painful? Which parts feel neutral, relaxed, free, open, or pleasant? We often get so caught up in our thoughts that we lose awareness of what is happening in our bodies. You may be surprised to discover that you have been unintentionally clenching your jaw or holding your breath. Alternatively, if you have been preoccupied by a headache or tight shoulders, you may not have realized until this moment that your legs feel pleasantly relaxed and pain-free. How does it feel to focus your attention on the body parts that feel good, even if just for a moment?

When you have finished your full body scan, spend a moment looking around the room or space you are currently in. Look up at the ceiling or sky, down at the floor or ground, and to either side. Turn all the way around in your seat and look behind you. See the furniture, objects, people, animals, and plants sharing space with you. Allow yourself to simply be present in this place and this moment. How does it feel to exist right here, right now? In this exact moment—not tomorrow, not tonight, not one second from now—are you safe?[2]

This is a simple exercise, but over time it can yield powerful results. When we become more attuned to our body—our sensations, our physical responses, our needs, and our preferences—we gain deeper clarity about the full picture of the mind-body-spirit connection. If you are new to this practice, you will be amazed to discover what simply becoming more aware, more present, and more grounded can do for your overall wellness! With this, we also become better equipped to self-soothe during difficult moments, which can build our capacity for the deep—and often scary and painful—work of healing the witch wound.

Other methods of soothing your nervous system and creating a foundation of safety in the body include breathwork, yoga, massage, mindfulness meditation, getting enough sleep, regular exercise or other forms of movement, balanced nutrition, and working with herbal plant allies. Practices that help you feel present in your body, such as dance, stretching, and self-touch, are also highly useful in this work.

Helping Emotions Flow Through Movement

Physical movement is a natural way for the body to process emotions and experiences, both positive and negative. Consider how the body instinctively responds when you receive exciting news: you may smile or even laugh, jump up and down, clap your hands together, or dance around with joy. Conversely, receiving negative news tends to collapse the body: you might sink into your chair, letting your shoulders round and your head drop forward into your hands. Unfortunately, most of us are taught to suppress these instinctual movements, which in turn stifles our emotional expression. When we are not able to process and express these heavy emotions, they can become stuck in the body.

The good news is that this emotional-somatic connection also works in reverse: we can tap into and move these stuck emotions by physically moving our bodies. Movement allows us to process suppressed feelings and energy, as well as access our deeper wells of creativity and intuition. It is important to note that intentional, healing movement is different from exercise. While running or lifting weights can certainly be cathartic and effective at moving stuck energy, there are other types of movement that are often even more effective. Two examples of this kind of mindful movement are dancing and stretching.

To practice moving stuck energy through dance, put on a soundtrack that speaks to you—if you need inspiration, search YouTube for "ecstatic dance music" or "spiritual music"—or simply dance in silence, allowing the rhythm of your own spirit to guide you. Close your eyes and allow your body to move freely in whatever way feels good. Start small by swaying your hips back and forth, then adding gentle shoulder movements. Float your hands away from your body, perhaps allowing them to drift upward and kiss overhead. Let your motions be fluid, easy, and intuitive as you find what feels good in your body. Feel into those body parts that are tight or constricted, such as your hips or chest. Allow your movements to grow bigger. Take up space.

You may find that this practice brings up feelings of sadness, anger, shame, guilt, or anxiety. If tears come, let them flow. On the other hand, you might find that you are able to tap into a feeling of personal power, creativity, or sensuality. There are no right or wrong experiences; every practice will yield something different. You can also use dance to work through your emotions during situations of turmoil or distress to ensure they do not become stuck within the body. I do this often when I run into a creative block while writing or when I feel my nervous system becoming dysregulated due to stress.

Stretching helps to move emotions through the body in a similar way. Hip and heart-opening stretches can be especially beneficial in the work of healing the witch wound. Find beginner-friendly stretches with instructions online, and hold each one for at least thirty seconds while breathing deeply and allowing your body to soften and relax into the pose. Stretching at the end of the workday has become a regular ritual for me, signaling to both body and mind that it is time to transition from productivity to rest and leisure.

Healing the Throat Energy Center

The throat energy center is related to our communication, self-expression, speech, creativity, and confidence. In chapter 8, we discussed how imbalances or blockages in the throat energy center can be a symptom of the witch wound. This energetic wounding can manifest physically with tightness, burning, or pain in the throat, but also in the form of feeling afraid to speak your truth and to express yourself authentically.

Unsurprisingly, speaking your truth is one of the most important things you can do to heal your throat energy center. Of course, this is often easier said than done—especially when you carry the witch wound and have a lifetime of people-pleasing behaviors behind you. Something I have found to be surprisingly effective in healing this part of myself is speaking my truth privately, to myself and only myself. Several years ago, I went through a period when I felt irritable, frustrated, and burned out nearly all the time. In retrospect, I can see clearly that these feelings were the result of poor boundary-setting skills and stifling my own self-expression for too long.

At the time, a particular card in my favorite oracle deck—Eruption—kept coming up again and again in all my readings. It felt like an apt warning: if I don't begin letting off some of this pressure, it's going to blow one way or another. So I began doing the only thing I could think of: anytime I felt that frustration, resentment, or anger bubbling up within me—the kind that was clearly the result of my boundaries being crossed or my needs going unmet—I would go outside into my backyard and just speak. "I feel annoyed, frustrated, mad, and bitter because my husband came into the kitchen when he knew I was taking an important work call there," or "I feel rejected, abandoned, lonely, and insecure because my friend didn't call me on the date they said they would."

Even though nobody was listening, it felt *so good* to use my voice to speak my truth and free those buried emotions from my body. Additionally, naming every emotion that I was experiencing out loud helped me gain a lot of clarity about what I was *really* feeling; *mad* is quite different than *agitated, resentful, fed up, furious,* or *exhausted.* In turn, this inner clarity made it much easier to communicate my true feelings to other people.

Positive affirmations—especially those related to communication and expression, such as "I speak my truth with confidence and ease" and "It is safe for me to express myself"—are also deeply healing for the throat center. Reciting an affirmation on a daily basis is a wonderful healing practice. Be sure to speak it out loud rather than simply reading it!

Other activities that can help heal this vital energy center are breathwork, chanting, humming, singing, and stretching through the throat and neck. In the Vedic tradition, HAM (pronounced like "hum") is the *bija* mantra or seed mantra associated with the throat chakra. Chanting HAM and allowing the sound to vibrate throughout your throat and jaw can help open, unblock, and balance your throat energy center.

This is far from the only sound you can use to heal this this energy center. Consider sacred symbols or words that are meaningful in your cultural heritage or spiritual tradition. For instance, modern druids can chant the three syllables of *Awen* ("ah – oh – en"), a Welsh word associated with divine inspiration in the druidic tradition. Followers of the Old Norse religion often chant or sing the names of the Elder Futhark runes, a practice known as *galdr*. Any of these sacred words can be used in a personal healing practice. You could even choose to chant the simple yet powerful affirmation "I am." Whatever word, mantra, or sound you are chanting, the key is to draw out the vowels and feel the vibrations physically.

Stretching the throat and neck can also stimulate the flow of energy through your throat center. Try this simple sequence of stretches right now: First, tilt your head so that your right ear drops toward your right shoulder. Hold this pose for three inhales and three exhales. If you need a deeper stretch, you can rest your right hand on top of your head, allowing the added weight to deepen the stretch without pulling or forcing. Slowly make your way out of the stretch—I like to use my right hand to push my head back into a neutral position—and repeat on the other side. Lastly, draw five slow, small circles with your nose in one direction, then in the opposite direction. You should feel a gentle stretch in different parts of your neck as your head moves.

BODY CONNECTION RITUAL

Many people, whether they are witches or not, have complicated relationships with their bodies. Like all living beings, our bodies shift and change with time. We are no different in that regard from the bear, whose body fat waxes and wanes with the seasons, or the ancient yew, who becomes increasingly gnarled and knotted as it ages. Why then do we humans expect our bodies to remain pristine and unblemished? Why do we demand perfection of ourselves when it is the imperfection of an asymmetrical mountain range, a crooked tree, or a speckled leaf that we find so beautiful and wondrous?

Body relationships can be further complicated by sexual trauma, chronic illness, injuries, and other past experiences that may leave us feeling betrayed by our own bodies. These experiences are valid and real—yet even imperfect, wounded bodies are deserving of love, tenderness, appreciation, and respect. Reconnecting with your body is an important step on the long and winding path of healing the witch wound. Why? The roots of this wound often run deep into our bones and tissues, and it is only by exploring our bodies that we can reach them.

This ritual invites you to simply hold space for the reality of your body by gazing at your own naked—or unclothed to your comfort level—reflection. I will not ask you to feel a certain way about your body, as painful emotions are just as valid as joyful ones. But I will invite you to stay open and to soften into the experience where possible.

Timing: After the sun has set.

Location: Anywhere with a mirror.

Tools: You will need a mirror you can stand in front of (ideally full-length, but a bathroom mirror will work too) and one or more candles (optional but highly recommended).

Before beginning the ritual, make any additional preparations you prefer—such as dimming the lights, playing meditative music, or lighting candles. For this ritual, I highly recommend turning off all overhead lights and working by lamplight or candlelight to create a sacred, sensual environment.

Then, energetically cleanse and bless your ritual space using your preferred method—such as burning incense, ringing a bell, or drawing out negative energy with a crystal. If you do not have any energy-cleansing tools available, you may visualize and sense a white ball of light glowing inside your solar plexus and expanding outward into a protective white sphere. Whichever method you use, state your intention to cleanse and protect your ritual space, thereby making it sacred and separating it from the mundane world.

When you are ready, open the ritual by closing your eyes and taking three deep, slow inhales and exhales, inviting your physical body to relax and any mental chatter to fade away.

Now, stand or sit so that you are facing your mirror and undress to your comfort level. I recommend performing this ritual fully naked, though you

       Heal the Witch Wound

may choose to leave your undergarments or any other layers on if you prefer. Trust your own intuition and do what feels best.

Once you have undressed, meet your own gaze in the mirror. Take in the reflection of your eyes, your forehead, your hairline, your nose, your mouth, your chin, and the shape of your face. Slowly, allow your gaze to lower across every inch of your body: your neck, chest, arms, hands, belly, groin, hips, legs, and feet (if you can see them in the mirror you are using). Notice every curve, freckle, birthmark, dimple, wrinkle, and scar. This is *you*. Take it all in.

Allow any and all emotions to surface, without holding them back: grief, joy, appreciation, shame, guilt, respect, anger, love. If you feel the need to cry, let your tears flow; if you feel the need to smile or laugh, do so freely. Resist any urge to judge yourself for your reactions. Instead, do your best to practice acceptance and nonjudgment for whatever comes up.

If it feels right, indulge in some gentle self-touch. Run your fingertips up and down your arms, across your shoulders, down your chest and belly, and along your legs. Experiment with varying pressures and types of touch. Explore, linger on the areas that feel good, and notice those that don't. The only goal here is to be present and connect with your own body.

Alternatively, you can begin to incorporate slow movements. Sway your hips, roll your shoulders, move your arms as if you were slowly drifting through deep, warm water. Appreciate the ways your body can move, and do what feels good.

Spend as long as you like gazing at your own reflection, being present with your body, and exploring the physical sensations of touch and movement. When you are ready to end the ritual, speak the following words out loud, directed toward your physical body:

> "Body, I am sorry for all the times I have been unkind to you, and I am grateful for all the things you enable me to do. I appreciate you. I honor you. I respect you. And I love you."

You may feel especially sensitive or vulnerable after this ritual. Follow it up by doing something that brings you comfort or joy, like watching your favorite feel-good movie or snuggling with a pet.

The spirit, body, and mind are all vital components of the self, and they are all connected. When one of these aspects of the self is unbalanced or unhealthy, it affects the others; the negative thoughts we hold about ourselves create physical tension in the body and neural pathways that reinforce those harmful beliefs. What's more, neglecting and suppressing your truth can make you feel both mentally and physically unwell. By taking a holistic approach to healing the body through exercises like positive affirmations, energy center healing, and releasing stored emotions, we weave a deep ancestral form of medicine that touches all layers of the witch wound.

15

Earth Healing

One of the most essential aspects of healing the witch wound is rebuilding and nurturing your connection with the sacred Earth. How would you describe your present relationship with the natural world? If you are like the majority of the Western population, you may have very little relationship to speak of at all. Over the past three hundred years since the Industrial Revolution reshaped the way we produce and consume goods, humans have become increasingly disconnected from the natural landscapes around us.

Many of us think of nature as some faraway thing: national parks where the land has been protected and preserved, a designated place that humans must travel to if they wish to interact with this thing called nature. In reality, this is a very narrow and disconnected view of nature—one that differs quite dramatically from how humans of the ancient past perceived it or how Indigenous cultures around the globe still regard nature today. Our ancestors knew that *we* are nature, and that therefore everything we do and everything that surrounds us is part of nature as well. The evidence of this is abundant, from the pre-Christian festivals that centered around the cyclical turning of the seasons to the folklore regarding burial mounds, ancestral spirits, fairies, and land spirits.

Animism is the belief or knowledge that everything has a spirit: animals, plants, trees, rocks, rivers, wind, mountains, forests, and other places. When we adopt an animistic worldview, there is no need to embark on lengthy treks to special locations to connect with the sacred Earth or with Spirit. The Divine exists all around us, all the time. It is alive in everything, everywhere—in the soil beneath your feet, in the skies above your head, in the herbs growing in your garden bed, and in the blood pumping through your veins. Animist belief reminds us that it's all nature and it's all sacred; that *we* are nature and *we* are sacred.

Certainly, I could board a plane or get in my car and travel to a national park to see majestic mountain ranges, canyons, and waterfalls or to spot whales, moose, or lions in their natural habitats. But are the blue jays that visit my backyard and the horseherb that grows through the cracks in my driveway not part of nature in equal measure? Of course they are—and they are waiting for me to step outside and connect with them in this very moment.

This sacred connection to the living Earth was stripped away from our ancestors by imperialism, colonialism, capitalism, and religious tyranny during the era of Christianization and again during the Burning Times. Our European ancestors in turn inflicted this same violence upon the people of the lands they colonized, denying them of their rights to Earth-based spiritual practices. Through centuries of spiritual taming, we lost connection with both Spirit and Earth, and instead turned our attention to more material pursuits. We learned to accumulate wealth rather than wisdom, to control the land beneath our feet rather than connect with it.

Yet Earth-based spirituality remains an innate part of each one of us. All we need to do to reclaim it is to embrace this sacred truth.

Attuning to the Cycles of Nature

The natural world has abundant lessons for us. Many of these center around how everything is born, lives, dies, and is reborn. From the changing of the seasons to the phases of the moon, we can witness a recurring cycle of growth and decay in all things related to the living Earth and the universe at large. This theme is wholly apparent in the Wheel of the Year—the calendar of festivals that many witches, pagans, and nature-based spiritual practitioners follow.

Whether you identify with one of these titles or not, celebrating the holidays of the Wheel of the Year—a modern calendar that is rooted in pre-Christian European religious practices and beliefs—is a powerful way to reacquaint your spirit with the rhythms of the natural world.

Samhain

November 1 in the Northern Hemisphere / May 1 in the Southern Hemisphere

According to the ancient Gaelic calendar, Samhain marked the end of the harvest season and the start of winter. It was also the time to guide cattle in from their summer pastures and slaughter some of them for the winter food supply. Samhain was believed to be a liminal time when the veil between worlds grew thin and portals to the otherworld were opened. Fairies, ancestors, and other spirits could pass through these portals and roam the lands. Bonfires were lit on the night of October 31, their flames and smoke serving to protect against baneful spirits. Because the Gaels believed darkness came before light (i.e., night before day and winter before summer), Samhain was also regarded as the start of the new year.

Yule / Winter Solstice

December 21–22 in the Northern Hemisphere / June 20–21 in the Southern Hemisphere

The winter solstice is the shortest and darkest day of the entire year, when we receive the least amount of sunlight. Yet as much as this is a time of darkness, it also marks the rebirth of the light. Each day following the solstice, the sun's power will grow little by little. This festival is therefore one of rest and reflection, but also new beginnings and creating our own light and warmth amid the cold darkness of winter. Many ancient cultures celebrated the winter solstice with feasting, drinking, singing, dancing, and gift-giving. These festivals were known by a long list of names, such as Saturnalia in Rome and Yule in Scandinavia.

Imbolc
February 1 in the Northern Hemisphere / August 1 in the Southern Hemisphere

Imbolc is one of the four Gaelic fire festivals, with the others being Beltane, Lughnasadh, and Samhain. Each of these four festivals marked the changing of the seasons—a phenomenon that was of vital importance to early agricultural societies. Imbolc is the festival that marks the coming of spring. While the days are still bitterly cold, the growing daylight delivers hope for new beginnings and future growth. It is celebrated as a date of both purification and fertility, as this was historically when ewes would begin producing milk. Imbolc is also associated with both Saint Brigid of Kildare and Brigid the pre-Christian goddess.

Ostara / Spring Equinox
March 19–21 in the Northern Hemisphere / September 21–24 in the Southern Hemisphere

Ostara is a modern pagan name for the spring equinox, which is often recognized as the first day of spring. On this day, light and dark are in perfect balance—yet the scales are preparing to tip. After this day, light will overtake the dark and continue to grow in strength until the summer solstice. The natural world is awakening from its winter slumber and preparing to give birth to new life. It is a time of balance, fertility, hope, and growth. The name Ostara is derived from Ēostre, who may have been a Germanic goddess of spring and the dawn.

Heal the Witch Wound

Beltane

May 1 in the Northern Hemisphere / November 1 in the Southern Hemisphere

For the ancient Gaels, Beltane marked the beginning of summer, when the cattle were driven out to their summer pastures. Sacred rituals were held to protect the cattle and the crops that had been planted earlier in the year. Great bonfires were lit across the countryside, and villagers would gather to feast, drink, and dance. Beltane folklore often centers around the themes of beauty and youthfulness, such as the belief that maidens who washed their faces with dew on the morning of Beltane would become more beautiful. This festival is largely associated with the greening of the natural world and the flourishing of life.

Litha / Midsummer / Summer Solstice

June 20–22 in the Northern Hemisphere / December 20–22 in the Southern Hemisphere

The summer solstice is the longest and lightest day of the entire year, when we receive the greatest amount of sunlight. It has been celebrated for thousands of years, likely since the start of the Neolithic era in 10,000 BCE. As ancient humans transitioned from hunter-gatherer to agricultural societies, they may have relied on the solstices and equinoxes to determine when to plant and harvest crops. The famous Neolithic monument Stonehenge is oriented toward the sunrise on the summer solstice. Also known as Midsummer or Litha, this is a day of vitality, abundance, and prosperity.

Lughnasadh / Lammas

August 1 in the Northern Hemisphere / February 1 in the Southern Hemisphere

Lughnasadh marks the midway point between the summer solstice and the autumn equinox. Agriculturally, this is when the fields are full of crops ripe for the harvest. This is a time to give thanks for the light, warmth, and abundance of the summer season, as well as to harvest the first grains and acknowledge the dying of the light. According to Irish mythology, Lughnasadh was established by the god Lugh as a funeral feast and athletic competition in honor of his foster mother Tailtiu. Traditional Lughnasadh celebrations have included visiting holy wells, artistic performances, and sporting competitions such as horse racing, running, hurling, spear throwing, archery, and wrestling.

Mabon / Autumn Equinox
September 21–24 in the Northern Hemisphere / around March 19–21 in the Southern Hemisphere

Mabon is a modern name given to the autumn equinox, which is often recognized as the first day of fall. Historically, this was a time for celebrating the bounty of the harvest season and preparing for the darkness of winter. It is a day of balance, harmony, gratitude, reaping, and fruitfulness. Traditional celebrations typically include feasting, singing, dancing, and decorating with fruits of the harvest. In some regions of Europe, the last sheaf of corn to be harvested was believed to have spiritual significance. This sheaf was woven into a corn dolly and replanted the following spring.

There are countless books, websites, and other resources that explore the origins, history, traditions, and symbolism of these festivals, as well as other ancient festivals that are not included in the Wheel of the Year. One of the simplest yet most meaningful ways to begin celebrating is by taking notice of what is happening in your local area on and around these holidays. Which plants are blooming? Which species of birds and other animals are appearing more regularly in your yard or favorite park? What time is the sun rising and setting each day?

You can also use these festival dates to look inward as well as outward. How are you feeling on Yule, the darkest day of the year? How are your energy levels and your mood? What responsibilities and hobbies are taking up most of your time? Are you feeling called to spend more time alone inside your home or out in the world with friends? How do the answers to these questions compare to your answers on Midsummer, the lightest day of the year? How do they compare to the other Wheel of the Year holidays? Because you are as much a part of nature as the landscape around you, it's quite possible that you will find you are affected by the cyclical rhythms of nature—if you simply take the time to notice.

Earth-Based Spiritual Practices

Just like the flora and fauna of this planet, we are of the Earth. For this reason, reconnecting with Earth does not need to be some big excursion or endeavor. Developing simple Earth-based spiritual practices and integrating them into your lifestyle can help you feel more connected, validated, held, understood, and at home in your body and on this planet. There are infinite ways to do this, but below are a few suggestions to get you started thinking about your relationship with the natural world.

Herbalism

Herbalism is the practice of studying herbs and other plants and using them to support wellness. It is an ancient craft—one that humans relied on for tens of thousands of years before the development of modern medicine. If you have ever sipped a cup of herbal tea before bed to help you sleep, then you have already experienced the benefits of plant medicine. Some witches study herbalism through designated training programs and go on to offer their tinctures and other herbal remedies as a full-time or part-time profession. But the truth is that anyone can study herbalism, and you can find most of what you need to know for free online and in books.

As a novice herbalist, sourcing your herbs from reputable online vendors like Mountain Rose Herbs or Starwest Botanicals is a good place to begin. You can find hundreds of varieties of dried herbs and spices on these sites, from echinacea and yarrow to valerian and elderflower. One of the simplest ways to start working with herbs is by preparing your own loose leaf teas at home. For instance, a blend of dried lavender, chamomile, and passionflower will yield a soothing cup of tea that you can sip before bed or when you need to de-stress.

As you become more familiar with herbs and their properties, you can venture into preparing infusions, tinctures, syrups, and other healthful concoctions. You could even start tending your own herbal garden at home! Building a personal relationship with the plants you use in your practice by caring for them with your own hands is one of the best ways to deepen your connection with the living Earth.

Herbalism is a path that is unique to every practitioner. While there are always safety considerations—for instance, it is a smart idea to research possible interactions with medications before working with a new herb—in general there are no rules about what it means to be an herbalist. The important thing is that you are building a relationship with plant allies and the sacred Earth—whatever that may mean to you personally.

Get Outside

In Japan, there is *shinrin-yoku* (forest bathing); in Norway, *friluftsliv* (outdoor life). Other cultures have their own terminologies, but ultimately the practice of connecting with the sacred Earth through time spent outdoors is something that is universal and does not require language. Have you ever looked up at a full moon and felt its light lift your spirits? Have you ever dug your toes into the sand and instantly been comforted and relaxed? Have you ever walked through a forest and fallen silent at the beauty and majesty of the natural world?

There is a reason why humans feel simultaneously awed and soothed by the natural world: because we recognize it, consciously or otherwise, as a place where we belong. Our own sacred and divine natures are reflected back to us by the wild, and that makes it feel like home. Spending time outside is a spiritual practice, whether that looks like a long hike on a local trail or sitting in an Adirondack chair in your backyard.

How frequently do you spend time outdoors? How much time does this add up to each week? When you do spend time outside, how present are you? There are no right or wrong answers to these questions. The idea is simply to become more mindful and intentional about your connection with nature. It's one thing to celebrate the pagan holidays on the Wheel of the Year, but another thing entirely to build a personal relationship with the land you live on. The best way to do that is by getting outside regularly and learning about your bioregion firsthand.

Communicating and Coregulating with Trees

One of my favorite practices for deepening my relationship with the land where I live is by connecting—physically, spiritually, emotionally—with trees. Yes, I am asking you to become a literal tree hugger! To do this, start by approaching a tree; you may choose a tree in your yard or in a local park or other outdoor area, but I recommend selecting a tree you can revisit easily. As you approach, ask the tree if you have permission to sit and spend time with it. You may experience a sense of simply knowing the answer, or you may need to wait for a sign like the leaves rustling in a sudden breeze. Trust—and respect—the initial answer you receive. No different than humans, some trees are more social and open to interaction than others.

Once you have permission, take a seat beneath the tree with your back pressed up against its trunk. If a seated position isn't comfortable, you can also stand facing the tree and place both hands against the trunk. Now, the active work is done—it is time to simply sit, observe, and listen. Let all mental chatter fade away and allow your senses to become attuned to the tree. Rather than closing your eyes, look around you; notice the texture and color of the bark, the light filtering through the leaves, the shape and size of the branches. Open yourself to any intuitive messages or emotions that may arise during this experience, but don't rely on them as a measure of success. The goal of this exercise is not purely to receive and gain insights, but rather simply to connect, spend quality time, and form a relationship with a nonhuman spirit.

With practice, you may discover that this action can have a profound impact on your mood, emotions, thoughts, and energy levels. That's because this is a form of coregulation—the process in which one person's nervous system helps to soothe, calm, and regulate the nervous system of another person, human or otherwise. Coregulation can be especially useful in moments of immense nervous system *dys*regulation, when self-regulation or self-soothing feels too difficult to manage. Try it out next time you are feeling stressed, overwhelmed, or overstimulated by noticing how it feels to attune to the energy of one of your favorite trees. You may find that this practice helps you feel more grounded, calm, and capable of navigating whatever challenge you are facing. Additionally, you can connect and coregulate with all kinds of nature spirits, such as other plants, stones, and bodies of water.

FOUR ELEMENTS RITUAL

Yet another way to nurture your relationship with the living Earth is by deepening your connection with the four classical elements: air, fire, water, and earth. These elements are present everywhere in the material world around us, but they also have profound spiritual meanings. A basic list of correspondences for each element includes these attributes:

- **Air:** East, spring, dawn, yellow, intellect, communication, inspiration, wit, memory
- **Fire:** South, summer, noon, red, creativity, passion, courage, willpower, transformation
- **Water:** West, autumn, dusk, blue, intuition, psychic abilities, empathy, wisdom, purification

- **Earth:** North, winter, midnight, green, structure, strength, stability, groundedness, safety

This ritual will help you attune to each of the four elements both within and around you. Note: These are commonly used correspondences in many modern witchcraft and pagan traditions, but they are not universal. If you associate the four elements with different directions or other attributes, feel free to use those instead.

Timing: Anytime. You will likely experience different results depending on the time of day as well as the season when you perform this ritual, so I recommend practicing it more than once to compare results.

Location: Outside.

Tools: None.

Begin the ritual in a standing or comfortable seated position, facing east. Close your eyes and take three deep, slow inhales and exhales, inviting your physical body to relax and any mental chatter to fade away. Then open your eyes and gaze out at the scene in front of you. What do you see that is representative of the element of air—a clear blue sky, fluffy clouds, birds flying overhead, or blades of grass fluttering in the breeze? Spend several moments focusing your attention on these details and notice what feelings or thoughts come up. How does it feel in your body, mind, heart, and spirit to connect with the element of air? Finally, reflect on the role of air in your own body by attuning to the sensation of breathing air in and out of your lungs. Consider how the act of breathing delivers fresh oxygen to your brain, allowing you to think and process the world around you, and how the air in your lungs enables you to speak. When you are ready to move on, bow your head and thank the air for its teachings.

Now, turn to face the south. What do you see that is representative of the element of fire—the sun blazing in the sky, light reflecting off metal or glass, fiery red or orange flowers blooming? Spend several moments focusing your attention on these details and notice what feelings or thoughts come up. How does it feel in your body, mind, heart, and spirit to connect with the element of fire? Finally, reflect on the role of fire in your own body by considering how your body creates its own heat. Every cell in your body generates heat as it burns up energy through chemical reactions, some more than others. Your blood then absorbs this heat and redistributes it throughout your body, regulating your temperature and allowing you to move, run, and dance. When you are ready to move on, bow your head and thank the fire for its teachings.

Now, turn to face the west. What do you see that is representative of the element of water—rain clouds in the distance, a lake or river, a birdbath full of water, morning dew, fog? Spend several moments focusing your attention on these details and notice what feelings or thoughts come up. How does it feel in your body, mind, heart, and spirit to connect with the element of water? Finally, reflect on the role of water in your own body by considering the fluids that your body produces—blood, urine, sweat, tears, saliva. These fluids protect sensitive tissues and organs, purge waste from your body, and respond to changes in your mood. When you are ready to move on, bow your head and thank the water for its teachings.

Now, turn to face the north. What do you see that is representative of the element of earth—a patch of soil, mountains or hills in the distance, gravel, stones? Spend several moments focusing your attention on these details and notice what feelings or thoughts come up. How does it feel in your body, mind, heart, and spirit to connect with the element of earth? Finally, reflect on the role of earth in your own body by considering how your bones and joints give shape and form to your body. Your bones enable you to stand, sit, and move, but they also protect vital organs and other tissues. When you are ready to move on, bow your head and thank the earth for its teachings.

When used regularly, all of the rituals and practices outlined in this chapter can help you nurture a deeper, more holistic relationship with the natural world. Yet ultimately, you do not need any rigid instructions or guidelines to accomplish this goal. As part of the living Earth, you are *always* one with nature—the key is simply to remain aware of that truth. By realigning how you view your relationship with the natural world, the way you think about your consumption of the Earth's resources will likely begin to shift as well. This is an important part of healing your capitalist and imperialist conditioning—two of the most insidious and harmful aspects of the witch wound, both for yourself and for the planet.

16

Moving into Your Magic and Power

Everything we have discussed thus far about healing the witch wound—clearing energetic blockages, calling in support and empowerment, working with ancestral healing, creating safety within your body, restoring the Divine Feminine, reconnecting with the sacred Earth—are important goals in their own right. But they are also stepping-stones toward the greater spiritual objective of reclaiming your power, honoring your magic, and embodying your authentic soul expression.

Your magic is your sacred birthright. It is yours to claim and yours to enjoy in all the ways you see fit. When you honor your magic as the sacred gift that it is—without fear, shame, guilt, or doubt—you heal yourself *and* the collective. This work is not easy, but it is deeply rewarding . . . and quite possibly, life-altering.

Coming Out of the Spiritual Broom Closet

In chapter 5, we discussed what it means to hide your magic "in the broom closet," and how this often looks like watering down the way you speak about your magic, dimming your own light, downplaying your spiritual beliefs and practices, hiding your intuitive gifts, and concealing your witchy nature. These behaviors are usually driven by fear, shame, guilt, and doubt, and while they may feel protective, they can actually *deepen* those painful feelings.

Although there is nothing inherently wrong with being secretive about your spiritual and magical practices—in fact, I strongly believe certain things *should* be for your eyes only—there is a difference between protecting your sacred acts and being forced to hide your magic out of fear. Do you long to be recognized and accepted for who you really are but the idea of rejection or persecution holds you back? This is an indication that your wounded inner witch is driving your behaviors. The goal is to allow your empowered inner witch to take over.

Coming out of the spiritual broom closet won't look the same for everyone, because not everyone starts from the same place, follows the same path, or faces the same challenges. To give just one example, let's say you are someone who privately identifies as a witch but can't fathom the idea of saying the words "I am a witch" publicly to anyone. That's okay—you don't have to, now or ever! There are many ways to ease yourself out of the broom closet that do not involve labeling yourself or your practice at all. This is true for anyone who walks any spiritual or magical path, whether the term *witch* resonates or not.

Right now, your capacity for being seen in your full magic and power might be small. Over time, though, you can build that capacity and gradually become more comfortable with being truly known. I have always been an introverted and private person, so when I first began dabbling in witchcraft and paganism, I kept *everything* to myself. When I realized that not allowing myself to be authentically seen was creating a disconnect between myself and those around me, I decided to start opening up little by little. I wasn't prepared to fully leave the broom closet, but I was ready to open that door.

My close friends and family members already knew that I practiced meditation, so I began sharing a few more details: "I'm meditating tonight because it's the full moon," or "I like meditating near my oak tree because it has a nice energy." Then I started displaying more of my crystals and other witchy items in my living room and kitchen rather than keeping them all on my altar or nightstand. I spent quite a while in this in-between phase, where people clearly knew I identified as spiritual but didn't know much beyond that point.

Then I started getting a little bit bolder. I remember the first time I left my small triple moon cauldron in the kitchen when my in-laws visited, and when I first wore my Elder Futhark rune earrings out to dinner with friends. In both instances, nobody noticed—or at least, nobody said anything. I also remember when I left a few witchcraft books on display in the living room, and a friend of a family member asked me point-blank if I was a witch. I responded with a wink, "Hah, I just might be!" It was a start.

Over time, I continued to open up: I posted pictures of my oracle cards on Instagram stories. I started talking about my full moon rituals in group settings. I told a friend about my plans to celebrate Samhain, then Yule. And I stopped disassembling my altar when guests came over. I also began answering questions about my beliefs more honestly and directly: Yes, I really do worship pagan deities. No, I don't work with demons, but I do work with land spirits. Yes, I practice witchcraft.

Through each of these changes, my behaviors were always a little bit ahead of my nervous system, but not excruciatingly so. I felt vulnerable and awkward, but not panicked or unsafe. I also gave myself adequate time for my nervous system to catch up between these phases of opening up. This allowed me to build my capacity for being seen in a way that felt manageable and tolerable.

Ultimately, there was never one major coming-out moment, but rather a natural unveiling of more parts of the real me. In other words, the eventual goal doesn't have to be saying the words "I am a witch"—it can simply be to align your inner and outer lives in such a way that if you *were* to embrace that title publicly, those who know you best would not be surprised.

Taking things slowly offers another benefit: it gives your friends and family time to process what you are sharing more gradually. This can be especially helpful if your loved ones have dramatically different spiritual or religious views compared to your own or if they have a history of being judgmental. On that note, you should never feel obligated to share your magic with people who are committed to misunderstanding you. Your magic is a sacred gift, and anyone who goes out of their way to shame you for that gift does not deserve to be blessed by it—at least until they are able to move past their own blocks and accept you for all that you are.

Examples: How to Speak about Your Magic to Other People

The specifics of these examples will not apply to every witch, pagan, or spiritual practitioner. Rather, they are meant to spark inspiration about how to communicate about your practices and respond during uncomfortable conversations.

When you are taking baby steps out of the broom closet:

- "I'm doing well, thanks for asking! I've been getting more into my spiritual practice lately, which has been making me really happy."

- "I can't hang out tonight because it's a full moon. Full moons are always my me-time."

- "I love crystals! I have a crystal collection at home; amethyst is my favorite stone."

- "I have been reading a book about Earth-based spirituality and am really enjoying what I'm learning."

- "Do you know anything about astrology? I have been learning to read my birth chart."

When you are ready to emerge a little bit more:

- "I had a nice weekend. It was the first day of spring, which is a date I always celebrate as part of my spiritual practice. How about you?"

- "Happy Halloween! I am celebrating Samhain, which is a Gaelic festival that predates Halloween. Have you heard of it?"

- "There is a new moon tonight, so I'll probably be setting some intentions and maybe doing a ritual. What about you?"

- "This is a pentagram necklace; I wear it for protection. It's a really meaningful symbol to me."

- "There is a metaphysical store downtown I would love to check out. Want to go look at witchy things with me sometime?"

- "I just started reading a new book about folklore, herbalism, and magical charms. It's very good so far."

When you're leaving the broom closet for good:

- "Yes, that is a book of spells. I use it a lot. There are some good ones in there!"

- "That's my ancestor altar. I use it for honoring and speaking with my ancestors."

- "I actually don't celebrate Christmas. I'm pagan, so I celebrate a winter solstice holiday called Yule."

- "That's a statue of Freyja. She is my patron deity, so I work with her often during rituals."

- "Yes, I am a witch! I have been practicing for about two years. Why do you ask?"

When you are dispelling misconceptions or responding to disapproval:

- "Actually, I'm pagan and the Devil has nothing to do with my practice. Equating all witches with Devil worship is a scare tactic that dates back to the witch trials."

- "Witches are not evil; they're just people like everyone else. Many witches actually use their magic to help other people."

- "I understand that you have a negative perception of witchcraft. But for the most part, my practice consists of making charms and doing spells for healing, protection, and personal growth. That's not very scary, is it?"

- "If practicing witchcraft has changed me at all, then it has changed me for the better. I feel happier, more connected, and more confident than ever before."

- "I know your religion is important to you. But I have my own beliefs, so I don't need to be reminded about what your religion says about magic. Those aren't my beliefs."

Trust Your Intuition

Have you ever been in a situation where you had a strong intuitive feeling about something or someone, but ignored that gut feeling because you didn't want to cause a scene or inconvenience anyone? Have you ever done this and later found out your intuition was exactly right? One of the most powerful things you can do to heal the witch wound is to practice trusting and honoring your intuition.

Is something telling you to take the long way home from work? Do you have a nagging feeling that you should check in on someone, grab the umbrella before leaving the house, or bring a jacket on your vacation even though the forecast is calling for mild weather? These small, everyday experiences *do* matter when it comes to nurturing your intuitive abilities. It's no different than developing any other skill. Regular practice and conditioning are the keys to success, and these seemingly insignificant moments are the perfect opportunity to strengthen your intuitive muscle.

Sometimes I like to test myself by speaking these thoughts out loud or writing them down when they come to me. It can be as minor as "there is an email from my client in my inbox right now" or as major as "my husband is going to be offered that job he applied for." The more I have opened myself to these subtle energies and messages, the more frequently my intuition has proved to be exactly right! Of course, my gut feelings aren't right 100 percent of the time, and yours likely won't be either. But in my experience, it's much better to act on your intuitive feelings and find out you were off the mark than to stifle your intuition—thereby eliminating any opportunity to practice and become stronger—out of fear of being wrong.

This advice also applies to your spiritual and magical practices. In fact, this is when trusting your own intuition becomes *most* important. Often, it is the fear of doing things the wrong way that causes us to hold back in our most deeply meaningful, magical work. We look to others—those with more education, experience, influence—to tell us what we can and cannot do with our own magic, our own power, our own connection to the Divine. We believe that our work lacks depth, meaning, and validity without the approval of these leaders.

Wise and magical soul, this could not be further from the truth. For tens of thousands of years, your ancient ancestors crafted their own spiritual practices, led by the whispered wisdom of their elders, the heartbeat of the land they lived on, and their inner voices. They were isolated from the world at large, confined to their local region with no access to books or internet or global gurus. Tell me—do you believe their practices lacked depth, meaning, and validity?

We have been taught that our own intuition is not enough to guide and protect us in our journeys of magic and spirituality, yet millennia's worth of spiritual tradition tells us otherwise. There are mistakes, imperfections, and opportunities for improvement, but there is no "wrong way." Make a promise to yourself to stop doubting your own spiritual and magical experiences. Stop second-guessing your visions and trance experiences, the messages you receive from dreams, the energy you sense, and the results of your divinatory readings. And if you are not already engaging in any of these practices, it's time to start.

Meditation is a foundational practice for strengthening your intuitive abilities. If you can't quiet your mind and navigate your own thoughts, how can you expect to draw meaning from any insights that may be coming through? If you are new to the practice, start small by committing to just one minute of meditation every morning. In my own experience, I have found that small daily practices are often more influential than longer, less frequent sessions. During this one minute, focus your attention on your breath and allow everything else to fade away. If you find your thoughts drifting—as they absolutely will do—simply notice and name the distraction, then bring your focus back to your breath. As you become comfortable with this new daily routine, work your way up to three minutes of daily meditation, then five, then ten, then twenty, and so on until you have developed a practice that feels fulfilling to you.

As with any skill, the more time and energy you put toward honing your intuitive abilities, the more you will reap the benefits of this work. Approach this process with openness, a sense of curiosity, and the wisdom that you are held and supported by a community of witches that stretches through time and across space. No matter what, you cannot fail.

Create an Empowered Witch Altar

Spend a few moments reflecting on all you have learned about the witch wound thus far—the atrocities of the Burning Times, the supposed crimes of suspected witches, and the myriad signs and symptoms we have discussed. By this point, you likely have a solid idea of which aspects of the witch wound you struggle with the most. These will likely be the same limiting beliefs, fears, and heavy emotions you chose to release in chapter 10's full moon ritual.

Now, consider the attitudes, beliefs, practices, people, and environments that will best support you in your journey to heal these particular scars of the witch wound. For instance, if your greatest obstacle is allowing yourself to be authentically known, you might benefit from calling in radical self-acceptance, trust that your closest loved ones will accept you for who you truly are, and inner strength to face the possibility of rejection. If your biggest pain point is fear of sharing your spiritual gifts with the world, you might consider calling in support from your well and wise ancestors, a safe space to share your gifts, and greater faith in your own magic.

As you reflect on the supportive beliefs, practices, allies, and energies you want to invite into your life, consider any symbols or spiritual tools that could be used to represent them. For example, rose quartz, rhodochrosite, and rhodonite are wonderful crystals for nurturing feelings of self-love and self-worth. Herbs like mint and basil are ideal for calling in financial success, wealth, and prosperity. The pentagram is a powerful symbol of protection and also represents the five elements of air, fire, water, earth, and spirit.

You will use these physical objects to create an Empowered Witch Altar—a sacred place you can visit to honor your inner witch and call in strength and support as you continue your healing journey. If you already have a spiritual or magical altar you use regularly, you can transform this space temporarily into your Empowered Witch Altar. Or you can construct a brand-new altar for this purpose. Personally, I enjoy having multiple altars. I use my main altar for my rituals and active workings, but I also like to construct goal-oriented altars I can visit to supercharge my intentions.

You may also decorate your Empowered Witch Altar with any objects that remind you of your own witchiness or that you feel epitomize spiritual and magical empowerment: cauldrons, candles, a besom (witch's broom), ancestral photos, your family tree, crystals, herbs, flowers, goddess or god figurines, and even images of real or fictional witches who inspire you.

In the early stages of your journey to heal the witch wound, you should commit to visiting your Empowered Witch Altar daily—yes, daily. All that is required is three minutes per day. I recommend visiting your altar at the same time each day to make it part of your routine; for many people, first thing in the morning or just before bed will be most convenient. It is up to you how you want to spend these three minutes each day; the important part is that you are at your altar connecting with your own magic and power in some way.

For instance, you might simply sit in quiet contemplation while gazing at the items you have decorated your Empowered Witch Altar with, reflecting on their meaning. Alternatively, you might light a candle and pray to your well and wise ancestors, deities, or highest self for guidance and support in the day ahead. You might also spend this time setting an intention for the day, pulling a daily tarot card, rune casting, journaling, meditating, or feeling gratitude for how far you have already come on your journey.

However you spend these three minutes each day, the ultimate result will be the same: by prioritizing this time for yourself, you show your wounded inner witch that you are on the path toward healing and nothing can hold you back from moving into your power anymore. By tapping into this mindset every day, you train your brain to create new neural pathways that will unlock the gates to deeper spiritual fulfillment and empowerment while strengthening your magical healing intentions.

Manifest Your Most Magical Life

If you *truly* lived in your full witchy power—if you banished limiting fears and beliefs, embraced your truest self, and lived the life of magic, fulfillment, creativity, success, and sacred connection you have always dreamed of—what would that life look like? As soon as you have finished reading the prompting questions below, take a moment to close your eyes and imagine this life in extreme detail.

What does it feel like to live in your full power? Are you a healer, a spiritual leader in your community, an artist, a business owner? Are you simply comfortable and confident in your own skin, regardless of your occupation? What does your home look like? Where is it located? How is it decorated? No detail is too small here—see your kitchen stocked with jars of dried herbs harvested from your garden or books you have written prominently displayed on your own living room bookshelf. What does the atmosphere or energy of your home feel like? What are you doing inside the home—are you resting and enjoying leisure time (perhaps with a good book and a cup of tea beside a crackling fire) or working hard to finish up a creative project or launch a new offering for your business? What do *you* look like? How are you dressed? How do you feel? What sort of energy is radiating from your aura in this image?

Right now, set a timer for five minutes. Spend these next five minutes imagining every possible detail of your most magical life—whatever that means to you. See the details of this life as clearly as possible, while also reflecting on the energy, emotions, and mood that come up as you fill in the narrative. Don't skip this exercise or quit before the five minutes are up! It is important to know what you are working toward as you progress in your healing journey, and visualizations can play a powerful role in manifesting your most magical life. Go ahead and complete this exercise right now, and consider repeating it before performing the ritual outlined in the next section.

NEW MOON RITUAL FOR EMPOWERMENT

Like the full moon, the new moon is a powerful time for performing magic. However, the energy of the new moon is especially potent when it comes to setting intentions and calling in positive changes. Each day after the new moon, the moon's light will grow little by little—and according to the principles of lunar magic, your intention will grow into fruition as well. In this ritual, you will craft a spell jar for self-empowerment. Spell jars work by drawing in and holding energies. By creating this spell jar on the new moon and activating it with your breath, voice, and chosen affirmation, you will have a powerful magical item that will help you keep the energy of empowerment close to you at all times.

> **Timing:** Perform this ritual on the new moon, ideally at night after the sun has set and the moon has risen—even though it will not be visible in the sky.

Location: I recommend performing this ritual outdoors under the night sky. However, this ritual can also be performed indoors or on a cloudy evening—simply open the curtains to ensure you have a view of the night sky, even though the moon itself will be invisible.

Tools: You will need an empty jar with a lid or cork, plus sea salt and rosemary for protection, bay leaf for success, basil for luck and prosperity, dried lemon peel for creativity and happiness, lapis lazuli for intuition and psychic abilities, clear quartz to amplify your intention, and cinnamon for an added boost of energy. You may further customize this spell jar by using any other ingredients that represent self-empowerment to you.

Before beginning the ritual, make any additional preparations you prefer—such as dimming the lights, playing meditative music, or lighting candles.

Then, energetically cleanse and bless your ritual space using your preferred method—such as burning incense, ringing a bell, or drawing out negative energy with a crystal. If you do not have any energy-cleansing tools available, you may visualize and sense a white ball of light glowing inside your solar plexus and expanding outward into a protective white sphere. Whichever method you use, state your intention to cleanse and protect your ritual space, thereby making it sacred and separating it from the mundane world.

When you are ready, open the ritual by taking a comfortable seat of your choice. Close your eyes and take three deep, slow inhales and exhales, inviting your physical body to relax and any mental chatter to fade away.

With your eyes still closed, reflect on the image of what your life would look like if you lived in your full witchy, magical, intuitive, embodied, creative power. More importantly, *feel* the emotions associated with this image: fulfillment, joy, love, pride, gratitude, excitement, or whatever else comes up for you.

Maintain this image in your mind's eye as you begin filling the jar with your ritual ingredients: sea salt, rosemary, bay leaf, basil, dried lemon peel, lapis lazuli, clear quartz, and cinnamon—or other ingredients as desired.

After you have finished filling the jar but before you have sealed it with the lid or cork, speak one of the following intentions directly into the jar, ensuring your breath flows into the container:

"I am a witch, and I am powerful."

"It is safe for me to be myself."

"I was born to live a magical life."

"I love and respect my spiritual gifts."

"I trust and honor my intuition."

"Magic brings infinite joy and happiness into my life."

"I speak my truth with confidence and ease."

"I attract those who accept me for who I truly am."

Then close the jar, and trust that it has been infused with your power and will. Keep the jar on your Empowered Witch Altar or in another safe location in your home. Whenever you feel your sense of self-empowerment waning, hold this spell jar in your hands and allow its positive energies to uplift and nourish your spirit.

In addition to using the above affirmations in this new moon ritual, you can also use them as part of a daily affirming practice. Remember, words cast spells! By reciting one or more of these affirmations on a regular basis, you breathe life and energy into them. Likewise, the more time you spend engaging with your Empowered Witch Altar and strengthening the image of your most magical life, the more powerful your intentions will become.

You heal the witch wound every time you lean into your magic, trust your intuition, honor your emotions, share your gifts, embrace your uniqueness, and open up about your practices. By celebrating your own magic and standing tall in your power—even when it is scary and uncomfortable, even when it changes the way you are viewed by other people—you break down those feelings of guilt, shame, and fear little by little. While it can feel extraordinarily difficult at first, over time your nervous system will begin to recognize that it is safe to be authentically you—and that is when the magic happens.

THE SPIRAL PATH OF THE WITCH

At last, magical soul, we have reached the end of our journey together. Through the pages of this book, we have voyaged through the dark history of the Burning Times, explored the pains of the witch wound, and begun the deeply healing work of tending these wounds with intention and care. We have woven these threads of past, present, and future into a holistic and soulful understanding of the witch wound that calls upon mind, body, heart, and spirit.

My hope is that these words have conveyed the power of emotional alchemy; that they have demonstrated how anxiety can be transmuted into curiosity, grief into empathy, loneliness into connection, and rage into passion. It has been an honor to guide you and to hold space for you on this journey—but now, trust that you are ready to move forward on your own.

The work of healing the witch wound is a lifelong process. Certain triggers will continue to feel uncomfortable and scary, but that does not mean you are stuck or not progressing. The path of healing is not a straight line, but rather, a spiral. You *will* circle back to the same lessons, thought patterns, emotions, and experiences again and again. Yet each time you arrive back at these old wounds, you come armed with new wisdom and experience. With time, you will discover that there is greater distance between those core wounds and your present self. They may still be a part of your life, but you will have more space to think, feel, and expand in new ways.

Even as I write these words, I can feel the parts of my wounded inner witch that still need tending—the parts of me that wonder if my voice matters, if I am worthy of the sacred role of writer, creator, guide. But if my words have touched even one soul, then I know this offering has served its purpose. Likewise, someone out there is waiting to receive *your* gifts right now. They are praying to hear your story, to witness your creativity, to behold your bravery, to feel your energy, to receive your magic, to revel in your truth.

This is what it means to walk the path of the witch: to claim your birthright of magic, step into your power, and enchant your inner and outer worlds—in doing so, to heal the energy of this planet we all call home. May you be divinely guided and protected on this path, wherever it leads you.

NOTES

Chapter 1

1. Silvia Federici, *Witches, Witch-Hunting, and Women* (Oakland, CA: PM Press, 2018), 15–19.
2. Heinrich Kramer and James Sprenger, *The Malleus Maleficarum of Heinrich Kramer and James Sprenger*, translated with Introduction, Bibliography, and Notes by Montague Summers (New York: Dover, 1971), 100–101.
3. Kramer and Sprenger, *The Malleus Maleficarum*, 121.
4. Anne Llewellyn Barstow, *Witchcraze: A New History of the European Witch Hunts* (San Francisco: HarperOne, 1995), 101.
5. Federici, *Witches, Witch-Hunting, and Women*, 19 and 27.
6. Thomas Wright, *A History of Domestic Manners and Sentiments in England during the Middle Ages* (London: Chapman and Hall, 1862; Project Gutenberg, 2019), *https://www.gutenberg.org*, accessed July 27, 2021, 438.
7. Federici, *Witches, Witch-Hunting, and Women*, 27.
8. Federici, *Witches, Witch-Hunting, and Women*, 29.
9. Federici, *Witches, Witch-Hunting, and Women*, 39–40.
10. Yvonne Owens, "The Saturnine History of Jews and Witches," *Preternature: Critical and Historical Studies on the Preternatural* 3, no. 1 (March 2014): 56; *https://doi.org/10.5325/preternature.3.1.0056*.

11. Nico Voigtländer and Hans-Joachim Voth, "Persecution Perpetuated: The Medieval Origins of Anti-Semitic Violence in Nazi Germany," *The Quarterly Journal of Economics* 127, iss. 3 (2012): 1346; https://doi.org/10.1093/qje/qjs019.
12. Owens, "The Saturnine History of Jews and Witches," 75.
13. Owens, "The Saturnine History of Jews and Witches," 71.
14. Kramer and Sprenger, *The Malleus Maleficarum*, 75.

Chapter 2

1. Bengt Ankarloo et al., *Witchcraft and Magic in Europe: The Period of the Witch Trials* (Philadelphia: University of Pennsylvania Press, 2002), 20–21.
2. Barstow, *Witchcraze*, 59.
3. Lara Apps and Andrew Gow, "Appendix: Johannes Junius: Bamberg's Famous Male Witch," in *Male Witches in Early Modern Europe* (Manchester University Press, 2003), 159–64; http://www.jstor.org.
4. Ankarloo et al., *Witchcraft and Magic in Europe*, 16.
5. Ankarloo et al., *Witchcraft and Magic in Europe*, 10–11.
6. Ankarloo et al., *Witchcraft and Magic in Europe*, 13, and Peter T. Leeson and Jacob W. Russ, "Witch Trials," *The Economic Journal* 128 (August): 2095–96; https://www.peterleeson.com.
7. Barstow, *Witchcraze*, 69.
8. Ankarloo et al., *Witchcraft and Magic in Europe*, 14.
9. Barstow, *Witchcraze*, 90.
10. W. N. Neill, "The Professional Pricker and His Test for Witchcraft," *The Scottish Historical Review* 19, no. 75 (1922): 209; http://www.jstor.org.
11. Barstow, *Witchcraze*, 131.
12. See both Barstow, *Witchcraze*, and Ankarloo et al., *Witchcraft and Magic in Europe*, for detailed (albeit differing) explanations of how these estimates were calculated, as well as how the myth of "nine million witches burned" came to be.

Chapter 3

1. Federici, *Witches, Witch-Hunting, and Women*, 18–19.
2. Federici, *Witches, Witch-Hunting, and Women*, 25.

3. Federici, *Witches, Witch-Hunting, and Women*, 29.

4. Federici, *Witches, Witch-Hunting, and Women*, 27 and 41.

5. Apps and Gow, "Secondary Targets? Male Witches on Trial," in *Male Witches in Early Modern Europe* (Manchester University Press, 2003), 45; *http://www.jstor.org*.

6. Ankarloo et al., *Witchcraft and Magic in Europe*, 43.

7. Apps and Gow, "Secondary Targets? Male Witches on Trial," 45.

8. Ankarloo et al., *Witchcraft and Magic in Europe*, 50.

Chapter 4

1. Federici, *Witches, Witch-Hunting, and Women*, 60.

2. Charlie Campbell, "How a 7-Year-Old Girl Survived Papua New Guinea's Crucible of Sorcery." *Time*, 16 July 2019; accessed November 5, 2021; *https://time.com*.

3. Federici, *Witches, Witch-Hunting, and Women*, 63.

4. Federici, *Witches, Witch-Hunting, and Women*, 52.

5. Alan Yuhas, "It's Time to Revisit the Satanic Panic," *New York Times*, 31 March 2021; accessed August 25, 2022; *https://www.nytimes.com*.

6. Aja Romano, "Why Satanic Panic Never Really Ended," *Vox*, 31 March 2021; accessed August 25, 2022; *https://www.vox.com*.

7. Yelena Dzhanova, "A Tennessee Pastor Led a 'Harry Potter' and 'Twilight' Book Burning," *Insider*, 6 February 2022; accessed August 25, 2022; *https://www.insider.com*.

Chapter 5

1. William L. Minkowski, "Women Healers of the Middle Ages: Selected Aspects of Their History," *American Journal of Public Health* 82, no. 2 (1992): 288; *https://ajph.aphapublications.org*.

2. Kramer and Sprenger, *The Malleus Maleficarum*, 74.

Chapter 8

1. Mark Wolynn, *It Didn't Start with You: How Inherited Family Trauma Shapes Who We Are and How to End the Cycle* (New York: Penguin Books, 2017).

Chapter 9

1. Kramer and Sprenger, *The Malleus Maleficarum*, 47.
2. Kramer and Sprenger, *The Malleus Maleficarum*, 66.
3. Caroline Heldman et al., "See Jane 2020 TV Report: Historic Screen Time & Speaking Time for Female Characters," Geena Davis Institute on Gender in Media, May 28, 2020, accessed October 7, 2021; *https://seejane.org*.
4. "The Double-Edged Sword of Online Gaming: An Analysis of Masculinity in Video Games and the Gaming Community," Geena Davis Institute on Gender in Media, accessed October 7, 2021; *https://seejane.org*.
5. "Public Opinions about Breastfeeding," Centers for Disease Control and Prevention, November 15, 2021; accessed October 7, 2021; *https://www.cdc.gov*.
6. Joyce Endendijk et al., "He Is a Stud, She Is a Slut! A Meta-Analysis on the Continued Existence of Sexual Double Standards," *SAGE Journals* (Dec. 2019); *https://journals.sagepub.com*.
7. Federici, *Witches, Witch-Hunting, and Women*, 40.
8. Kramer and Sprenger, *The Malleus Maleficarum*, 46.

Chapter 11

1. Michael Lipka and Claire Gecewicz, "More Americans Now Say They're Spiritual but Not Religious," Pew Research Center, September 6, 2017; accessed October 12, 2021; *https://www.pewresearch.org*.

Chapter 13

1. Brian Handwerk, "An Evolutionary Timeline of Homo Sapiens," *Smithsonian Magazine*, 2 February 2021; accessed September 7, 2022; *https://www.smithsonianmag.com*.
2. Leften Stavros Stavrianos, "Relations Between the Sexes Were More Equal During the Paleolithic Millennia than at Any Time Since," in *A Global History: From Prehistory to the Present* (Englewood Cliffs, NJ: Prentice Hall, 1991), 9.
3. Barbara Tedlock, *The Woman in the Shaman's Body: Reclaiming the Feminine in Religion and Medicine* (New York: Bantam Books, 2006).

4. Helen Benigni, *The Mythology of Venus: Ancient Calendars and Archaeoastronomy* (Lanham, MD: University Press Of America, Inc., 2013).
5. Michael Balter, "Did Sexual Equality Fuel the Evolution of Human Cooperation?" *Science*, 14 May 2015; accessed August 29, 2022; *https://www.science.org*.

Chapter 14

1. You can also find many free supportive resources online. A few of my favorite Instagram resources for nervous system healing are @the.holistic.psychologist, @holistic.life.navigation, @repairing_the_nervous_system, @ablackfemaletherapist, @somaticexperiencingint, @nedratawwab, @somaticloveandhealing, and @haileypaigemagee.
2. I was taught this exercise by somatic therapist and educator Luis Mojica during his six-week course "Releasing Stress & Trauma Through Listening To Your Body." Learn more about Luis and his work at *www.holisticlifenavigation.com*.

BIBLIOGRAPHY

Ankarloo, Bengt, et al. *Witchcraft and Magic in Europe: The Period of the Witch Trials*. Philadelphia: University of Pennsylvania Press, 2002.

Apps, Lara, and Andrew Gow. "Appendix: Johannes Junius: Bamberg's Famous Male Witch." In *Male Witches in Early Modern Europe*, 159–66. Manchester University Press, 2003. Accessed July 27, 2021. *http://www.jstor.org*.

———. "Secondary Targets? Male Witches on Trial." In *Male Witches in Early Modern Europe*, 43–64. Manchester University Press, 2003. Accessed August 12, 2021. *http://www.jstor.org*.

Barstow, Anne Llewellyn. *Witchcraze: A New History of the European Witch Hunts*. San Francisco: HarperOne, 1995.

Balter, Michael. "Did Sexual Equality Fuel the Evolution of Human Cooperation?" *Science*, 14 May 2015. Accessed August 29, 2022. *https://www.science.org*.

Benigni, Helen. *The Mythology of Venus: Ancient Calendars and Archaeoastronomy*. Lanham, MD: University Press Of America, Inc., 2013.

Campbell, Charlie. "How a 7-Year-Old Girl Survived Papua New Guinea's Crucible of Sorcery." *Time*, 16 July 2019. Accessed November 5, 2021. *https://time.com*.

Dzhanova, Yelena. "A Tennessee Pastor Led a 'Harry Potter' and 'Twilight' Book Burning." *Insider*, 6 February 2022. Accessed August 25, 2022. *https://www.insider.com*.

"The Double-Edged Sword of Online Gaming: An Analysis of Masculinity in Video Games and the Gaming Community." Geena Davis Institute on Gender in Media, 17 Aug. 2021. Accessed October 7, 2021. *https://seejane.org.*

Endendijk, Joyce J., et al. "He Is a Stud, She Is a Slut! A Meta-Analysis on the Continued Existence of Sexual Double Standards." *SAGE Journals*, 27 Dec. 2019. Accessed October 7, 2021. *https://journals.sagepub.com.*

Federici, Silvia. *Witches, Witch-Hunting, and Women.* Oakland, CA: PM Press, 2018.

Handwerk, Brian. "An Evolutionary Timeline of Homo Sapiens." *Smithsonian Magazine*, 2 February 2021. Accessed September 7, 2022. *https://www.smithsonianmag.com.*

Heldman, Caroline, et al. "See Jane 2020 TV Report: Historic Screen Time & Speaking Time for Female Characters." Geena Davis Institute on Gender in Media, 28 May 2020. Accessed October 7, 2021. *https://seejane.org.*

Historic England. "Field Systems: Introductions to Heritage Assets." Historic England, 2018. Accessed August 5, 2021. *https://historicengland.org.uk.*

Kramer, Heinrich, and James Sprenger. *The Malleus Maleficarum of Heinrich Kramer and James Sprenger.* Translated with Introductions, Bibliography, and Notes by Montague Summers. New York: Dover, 1971.

Leeson, Peter T., and Jacob W. Russ. "Witch Trials." *The Economic Journal* 128 (August 2017): 2066–2105. Accessed July 30, 2021. *https://www.peterleeson.com.*

Lipka, Michael, and Claire Gecewicz. "More Americans Now Say They're Spiritual but Not Religious." Pew Research Center, 6 Sept. 2017. Accessed October 12, 2021. *https://www.pewresearch.org.*

Minkowski, William L., MD. "Women Healers of the Middle Ages: Selected Aspects of Their History." *American Journal of Public Health* 82, no. 2 (1992): 288–95. Accessed July 30, 2021. *https://ajph.aphapublications.org.*

Neill, W. N. "The Professional Pricker and His Test for Witchcraft." *The Scottish Historical Review* 19, no. 75 (1922): 205–13. Accessed July 30, 2021. *http://www.jstor.org.*

Owens, Yvonne. "The Saturnine History of Jews and Witches." *Preternature: Critical and Historical Studies on the Preternatural* 3, no. 1 (2014): 56–84. Accessed November 2, 2021. *https://doi.org.*

Palframan, Jef R. "Frost Witches: The Spark of the Bamberg Witch Craze." *Oglethorpe Journal of Undergraduate Research* 2, iss. 1 (2013). Accessed December 22, 2012. *https://digitalcommons.kennesaw.edu.*

"Public Opinions about Breastfeeding." Centers for Disease Control and Prevention, 15 Nov. 2021. Accessed December 23, 2021. *https://www.cdc.gov.*

Romano, Aja. "Why Satanic Panic Never Really Ended." *Vox*, 31 March 2021. Accessed August 25, 2022. *https://www.vox.com.*

Stavrianos, Leften Stavros. *A Global History: From Prehistory to the Present.* Englewood Cliffs, NJ: Prentice Hall, 1991.

Tedlock, Barbara. *The Woman in the Shaman's Body: Reclaiming the Feminine in Religion and Medicine.* New York: Bantam Books, 2006.

Voigtländer, Nico, and Hans-Joachim Voth. "Persecution Perpetuated: The Medieval Origins of Anti-Semitic Violence in Nazi Germany." *The Quarterly Journal of Economics* 127, iss. 3 (2012): 1339–92. Accessed November 2, 2021. *https://doi.org.*

Walker, Pete. *Complex PTSD: From Surviving to Thriving.* New York: Azure Coyote, 2013.

Wolynn, Mark. *It Didn't Start with You: How Inherited Family Trauma Shapes Who We Are and How to End the Cycle.* New York: Penguin Books, 2017.

Wright, Thomas. *A History of Domestic Manners and Sentiments in England during the Middle Ages.* London: Chapman and Hall, 1862; Project Gutenberg, 2019. Accessed July 27, 2021. *http://www.gutenberg.org.*

Yuhas, Alan. "It's Time to Revisit the Satanic Panic." *The New York Times*, 31 March 2021. Accessed August 25, 2022. *https://www.nytimes.com.*

TO OUR READERS